THE ANACH

OF TI.

THE ANACHRONISM OF TIME

A Theological Study into the Nature of Time

IAIN M. MacKENZIE
Canon Residentiary of Worcester

The Canterbury Press
Norwich

© Iain M. MacKenzie 1994

First published 1994 by The Canterbury Press Norwich
(a publishing imprint of Hymns Ancient & Modern Limited,
a registered charity)
St Mary's Works, St Mary's Plain,
Norwich, Norfolk, NR3 3BH

*Iain MacKenzie has asserted his right under the Copyright, Designs
and Patents Act, 1988, to be identified as Author of this Work.*

British Library Cataloguing in Publication Data

A catalogue record for this book is available
from the British Library

ISBN 1–85311–089–2

*Typeset by Datix International Limited
Bungay, Suffolk and
Printed and bound in Great Britain by
St Edmundsbury Press Limited
Bury St Edmunds, Suffolk*

For my dear Wife and Children, Lynne, Rorie, Ewen and Morag, and in loving memory of my Parents, Brothers and Sister.

Contents

Foreword

by Professor Thomas F. Torrance

THIS IS a quite remarkable book in which we are given an original and refreshing account of *time* from a distinctively theological perspective, and specifically in relation to 'the fulness of time' which God has for us in the incarnation when he sent his Son made of a woman into our world of space and time. In a discussion of Grosseteste's question whether or not the incarnation would have taken place had there not been a fall of man, Canon MacKenzie answers it in the affirmative for neither the incarnation nor redemption can be regarded as some kind of divine after-thought. There follows an examination of the interrelation of the incarnation and creation in which considerable use is made of Irenaeus's concept of the recapitulation of all things and all time, with its implication that in the beginning as in the end all things are present to God. This gives rise on the one hand to a deeper understanding of the creation in terms of what the author calls a 'double contingence', to and from God, the dependence and yet the freedom of creation. And this leads on the other hand to a deeper conception of eternity as 'a dynamic Present', and to a rejection of any notion of 'eternity' as 'endless time' or as 'timelessness'. Prompted by Grosseteste's scientific concern with the behaviour of light and his theological insight into its nature, Iain MacKenzie uses throughout the illustration of the single beam of light which is refracted into its constituent colours. The single beam of light is the uncreated Light of God, but we pass through the refracted colours as through ages, centuries, years, months, minutes, yet the beginning and the end are present to God, for all created time is embraced and upheld by the uncreated time of God's eternal Life. Our life and death, our time and what we are in our time, are affirmed by their fulfilment in the Time of God concentrated like his eternal Love in the Incarnation, for the time of Jesus Christ is the time which God has for us and makes for us in assuming our humanity upon himself.

One of the very interesting features of this work is the way in which the author wrestles with the history of ideas at decisive points, for example in the *Hexaemeron* of St Basil, in order to trace pointers throughout the development of Christian thought to a better understanding of what we perceive as 'time'. He constantly stresses that when we think and talk of 'time' we are concerned not with quantitative measurement, as in the natural sciences, but with real time as a dynamic quality of existence, with time as it 'is', 'has become' and always will be'. From a theological point of view this is to be grasped properly only in Christ who as God become man is the First and the Last, the Beginning and the End.

Apart from being devoted to the clarification of the nature of time, this is a book about the nature of theology. This is apparent not only in the account given in the Prologue about theological thinking determined or governed by its proper object, and therefore about the regulative role of Christology in theology, but all through in the critical and restrained way in which MacKenzie handles theological relations and concepts. Of special note is the way in which he bends ordinary terms to match the nature of divine reality, as for example in his steady cutting back of the spatial and temporal content carried in our ordinary language when we deploy it theologically to speak of divine presence and activity. We may not project our spatial or temporal relations into God.

Canon MacKenzie holds theological statements to be 'para-deigmatic' in character, for by their nature they do not encase the truth within themselves but direct us to the truth beyond themselves. Hence in a disciplined theology we operate with terms that are stretched beyond their normal usage and are adapted appropriately to their proper object, the fact and event and Person of the Word made flesh. In such a careful usage of temporal language, which is all we have, we can construct pointers to that which is more than time as we experience it. In this way MacKenzie does engage in what one might call 'holy speculation' as he seeks to press his thinking beyond the boundaries of what has been explicitly revealed by God, but he does so with a holy restraint and humility in the recognition of the principle of Grosseteste that all our infinities are finite to God.

While definite theological statements abound throughout his book, the author insists that they must not be taken in a final sense as conclusions. Indulgence from the reader is requested for them, for they have been made under the proviso of the awareness of the impropriety of all language when it is directed to that which is beyond this created dimension in which we live and move and have our being, and think and talk and write. We see through a glass darkly. No conclusions are therefore actually formulated in this book. What statements are made are to be construed as but goads to further thoughts. No one will, perhaps, find himself or herself in agreement with all the statements made in this work, but there is little doubt that in it Canon MacKenzie has done a great service in lifting theological understanding of time on a higher level where unhurried meditation upon what he has written will prove very rewarding.

T.F.T.

ACKNOWLEDGEMENTS

ANYONE who undertakes any level of academic endeavour knows that there are ever widening circles of people to whom he or she owes thanks. Indeed the prayer 'for our benefactors known and unknown' is applicable in such matters. So wide is the circle of those who have influenced and helped and without whom the undertaking would not have come to fruition, that it is beyond the most well-intentioned capability to mention them all. From home, through schooldays, universities, parishes, appointments, up to the more immediate circumstances around the actual production of the work, there is a veritable host of such influences – parents, schoolmasters, tutors, professors, colleagues and friends.

For me, the common sense Christian influence of my parents is the basis of all. From there many persons spring to mind and, out of that host, those concerned with the immediate production of this work. Even here one has to go back a few years, for I cannot forget the love of patristics instilled by Bishop David Jenkins, when he was Chaplain and Fellow of The Queen's College, Oxford, nor the same love of an excitement in systematic theology by the Very Reverend Professor T. F. Torrance when he was Professor of Christian Dogmatics in the University of Edinburgh. To the latter I also owe much encouragement as my thinking about time evolved and as this came to its present (but by no means final) fruition. I thank him for the time he has taken in the midst of a still very busy and productive life, to read my typescript and write a most generous foreword to this book. Such is his generosity of mind that he has been more than kind to me over the points on which I could not expect his total agreement.

As to the progress of the work, I single out, and by no means exhaustively so, several persons who have made my task lighter: my Assistant Librarian in Worcester Cathedral, Mr R. Stratton, who made several suggestions regarding mediaeval manuscripts and translations – and searched diligently; Dr B. S. Benedikz, whose wealth of learning has been a well for me from which to draw; Dr Joan Greatrex, whose erudition in mediaeval studies gave me many a direction towards which to look; Mr James Wood, formerly Rhodes Scholar, Worcester College, Oxford, for his scrutiny and comments; Mr F. Rawlings, who read over my typescript and corrected many of what are euphemistically called 'typing errors'; Mr C. Rawlings, formerly of St Chad's College, Durham, and now of the British Council, who made many valuable suggestions from his field of zoology; Mrs J. Barnes in the Worcester Chapter Office, who in her own time has assisted in so much of those mechanics which surround any possible publication; and Mr Giles Gasper of Christ Church, Oxford, who has, from the discipline of historical studies, been a constant encouragement and help.

I have been more than assisted in all this work by the loving understanding of my wife and children when my sorties into the study in the midst of all the duties of a Canon Residentiary made me somewhat preoccupied and out of circulation on many occasions. Their constant interest has been a mainstay to me. To my colleagues, the Dean and Chapter of Worcester and, indeed, to the congregations of the Cathedral, I also owe thanks for their theological charity when the subject of Time invariably crept into my sermons.

To the Reverend Gordon Taylor, Rector of St Giles-in-the-Fields, London WC2, also goes my gratitude for inviting me to give the lectures in the annual series at St Giles in 1992, out of my text, then in embryonic preparation. His hospitality in so doing, and the feed back I had from the large number of people from a wide area of England who attend these series, helped me greatly in the final formation of this work.

The use of the word 'man' or 'mankind' in the text is generic in keeping with the original texts and is not to be construed as exclusive language.

In the immediate production of this book, I am grateful to Morag Reeve of Darton, Longman and Todd, Auriol Milford of Oxford University Press, Dr Geoffrey Green of T. and T. Clark, Edinburgh, Linda Nichol of Cambridge University Press, and James Rivington and Hilary Kent of the British Academy, for their helpfulness and advice over permissions to use quotations from publications from those presses recorded in the Notes, and for the permissions granted by these Publishers; also my thanks are due to the British Academy for permission to quote from the

Dales and Gieben text of Robert Grossetestes's *Hexaemeron* published for the British Academy by Oxford University Press in 1982. They have all shown generous and ready assistance in the matter. The version of Psalm 90 at the conclusion of the book is that of Coverdale, 1535. Extracts from the Authorised Version of the Bible (The King James Bible), the rights in which are vested in the Crown, are reproduced by permission of the Crown's patentee, Cambridge University Press.

To Mr Kenneth Baker and his colleagues in The Canterbury Press Norwich, I owe a substantial debt of gratitude for the kindness, encouragement and assistance in all the manner of ways that I have experienced from them in the acceptance and publishing of this work.

IAIN M. MACKENZIE

That which hath been is now;
and that which is to be hath already been;
and God requireth that which is past.

Ecclesiastes 3:15

Thou art the true refulgence of the sun,
Radiant above the stars, and from thyself
Illuminest for ever all the tides of time,
. . . God indeed begotten of God,
Thou Son of the true Father, wast from aye.

To Christ our Lord: Cynewulf

Prologue

ALL who write about time must be humbled by the object of their endeavours. We are creatures of time; we cannot stand outside it and view it dispassionately. Inevitably, our existence, who we are, what we are, and our experiences, what we have been through, what our hopes are, will colour in the deliniations of what we think about time. In any case, whatever we write or say about time will pass into time's maw, and may be ruminated on later by those who follow in time, or not, as the case may be.

This is a work about time, written by me in my time, from my perspective. That is a subjective statement; but it is objectively realized. I know in part, in the writing of it, to whom I owe debts for whatever erudition may be mine. But I also know in the other part that I am the recipient of benefactors whose names I know not – names long forgotten by me, and names that history has not recorded, but whom eternity, the fulfilment of time, will reveal – my benefactors unknown.

Even here is a statement which is of personal belief, but it is made on the objective realization that I am the product of many people of the past, and who are contemporaries. Am I also the inheritor of those who are yet to come? I do not exist in a vacuum. I am not disenfranchised. I have a community to which I am indebted. It is that known and that unseen cloud of witnesses who have made me what I am, and whose voices inevitably echo in all that I say or write.

As one who confesses theology, I can only but follow out the rules of my discipline – otherwise I become a vagabond, picking up bits and pieces by way of wandering trespass on other folks' preserves, and end up a wayward thinker festooned with others' thoughts in tawdry disarray.

The way between Theology and what is called 'Science' is so peopled. Perhaps, because the way is easier and trespass notices not so carefully placed, there are many more travellers purporting to have come from Theology seeking the gleanings of Sociology, Educational Theory, Politics, and all the rest which claim the label of 'humanities and sciences' – a farther reach and narrower bend of the original demarcation of the words. Amongst these I do not want to be numbered. Generally (though not all of them) they stand in the shadow of the more dubious and deistic strands which is still cast from that curiously named 18th century episode, the Enlightenment.

It is a hallmark of such followers of a withered deism and outmoded rationalism, that they have little to say which is constructive about time and human existence. Convenience and expediency, both financial and social (and sometimes financial as opposed to social and social as opposed to financial) and their varied visions as to how to bring about the happiness of society, that Benthamite hollowness, are their mainspring. Time and human existence are subservient to these.

I stand with those who see the word 'Science' as indicating a particular field of learning, in other words, a specific discipline, and who operate by the ways dictated by the object of their study. Their attitude of mind and their subsequent terminology, will be dictated by the nature of that object as appropriate to what it is in itself. This is the hallmark of what is truly 'Science'.

Theology is itself a 'Science'. It looks at the objective facts of the revelation of God, and follows these in its thoughts and in the way it expresses itself. It is not subject to any other consideration, however plausible or popular. It is not mastered by any but by God before Whom it is faithful.

Indeed, there are many gods and many devotees. It is my contention that Theology and proper Science follow the one and the same Objective. They are not subject to cultural relativity, expediences, whims of fashion in all areas of thought, and the compromises which it may be temporally popular to take note of from these. Unfortunately, the declarations from so many 'experts' are based on such, and this has resulted in the phenomena of the pseudo-sciences.

Theology and Science, properly called, are both concerned with this existence of ours in what may be described as this world of time and things. But not in such a way that their content is prescribed and proscribed from within the milieu in which they operate, namely the circumstances and needs expressed of society as we experience them. That is not to say, and this must be emphasised, that they are concerned with 'timeless' truths. On the contrary, they are indeed concerned with truths which speak out to our time, and are firmly anchored in this dimension of the reality of our existence in which we live and move and have our being.

It is the firm anchoring of these for which there should be mutual concern. Otherwise they cannot speak out with any authority, save that of the passing public demand for assurance of what the public wants.

In order to be of proper service, Theology and Science have to be (in the old meaning of the word) 'disinterested'. That is not to say detached from reality; rather, speaking out of reality from a vantage point without fear or favour, so that reality is informed and may reform itself.

This vantage point is variously seen by Theology and Science, but not necessarily exclusively so – unless by blinkered parties on both sides. The legacy left by such blinkered Theologians and squinting Scientists throughout the ages, should, in the common good, be renounced, and a new inheritance formulated for future generations, drawn up by mutual respect.

It is good to see the tribute paid by Coveney and Highfield in *The Arrow of Time*[1] to those in other disciplines who have spoken and written about time, and their citation of Eddington[2] that:

> In any attempt to bridge the domains of experience belonging to the spiritual and physical sides of our nature, time occupies the key position.

Here at least is an admission in a scientific work that the question of time is best served variously from different disciplines.

In all that follows we will be looking at time from a theological standpoint, but with an eye to what our colleagues in the various scientific disciplines are saying and have said on the matter. This is not an artificial cover up in order to walk hand in hand and cry 'peace' when there is no peace, a Rite A rubric foist on people, but an attempt from the integrity of theology to offer whatever out of that treasure house of the ages might be of value towards a mutual understanding of time and of human existence therein.

It is – as every work on time must be – but an attempt and only an attempt. We see, as the Apostle Paul warns us, but through a glass darkly. We are not yet in that position – and never will be in this dimension of time – to see fully and face to face.

Professor T. F. Torrance has warned me that all thinking about time is tangential. That is to say we can never arrive at the point of finality about time, and think we have solved the problem. That of course is abundantly true, but at least we can venture (though not without compass) farther along the line towards its touching of the circle and perhaps glimpse more than others who would not and have not trodden so far. If I have gone farther than he would have wished me, at least he has provided me with that compass (and how grateful I am to him for that time-tried and reliable instrument of theological direction). Any straying into precipitous paths and labyrinthine ways is due to my misreading of it. But go on we must. Theology does not stop, and as for its endeavours – well, as after Gamaliel's observation,[3] if it is of God it will stand, if not it will fall.

And so I offer these observations on time. I have made use of the hospitality of the wisdom of some great figures of the past – such as I see endeavouring to press on to things which they could not express. If I have taken the generosity of their wisdom and mis-spent them on the way, I can only say that I hope to be given, by the grace of God, the opportunity to apologize to them when time is fulfilled and we see all face to face.

Likewise, I hope that others will take up where I have had to leave off, and strive yet farther along the way of understanding the God Who has come into time and understands us, the workmanship of His hands.

Whatever anyone may construe out of this work, I would place before all who read it, the thoughts of two diverse persons, different in their times, but both saying from opposite ends what they feel about time and their existence.

The first is the seventeenth century divine, Thomas Traherne,[4] who in his time could write about this selfsame part of the country in which this presently is being written:

> When I see a little church environed with trees, how many things are there which mine eye discerneth not. The labour of them which in ancient ages builded it; the conversion of a kingdom to God from paganism, its protection by laws, its subjection to kings, its relation to bishops, its usefulness and convenience for the entertainment of Christians, the divine service, the office of ministry, solemn assemblies, praises and thanksgivings, for the sake of which it was permitted, is governed, standeth and flourisheth.

Perhaps when I look upon it, it is desolate and empty almost like a heap of stones, none of these things appearing to the eyes which nevertheless are the spiritual beauties which adorn and clothe it. The uses, relations, services and ends being the spiritual and invisible things that make any material to be worth.

He who cannot see the invisible cannot enjoy nor value temples. But he that seeth them may esteem them all to be his own and wonder at the divine bounty for giving them so richly.

So it is with time and how we look at it. We may see the wrecks of time, the desolation of generations and the wasteland of past human folly and apprehension about and fear for the future. But that is to look on the surface. From the theological vantage point of time related to the Creator of all in Jesus Christ, the inner content and hidden meaning of time may become apparent – that is when time is looked at, inasfar as we can, in its context. Rather as in a child's kaleidoscope, the first surface view is of jumbled chaotic shapes and colours, so viewed properly the most beautiful and harmonious patterns emerge. So too, a surface view of time may exhibit but little of its significance. But so too, conversely, a surface view of time may give rise to a sense of security – 'I am the master of my soul and the captain of my salvation' – and we do not perceive that the radiant glow of such a sense of mastery over time is touched and distilled by the alchemy of death.

But there is a certainty about our existence in time which is legitimate, in looking realistically at time, and this best summed up by the second writer I cite, John Campbell Shairp (1819–1895) in his hymn:[5]

'Twixt gleams of joy and clouds of doubt
  Our feelings come and go
Our best estate is tossed about
  In ceaseless ebb and flow.
No mood of feeling, form of thought,
  Is constant for a day;
But Thou, O Lord, Thou changest not:
  The same Thou art alway.

I grasp Thy strength, make it mine own,
  My heart with peace is blest;
I lose my hold, and then comes down
  Darkness and cold unrest.
Let me no more my comfort draw

From my frail hold of Thee,
In this alone rejoice with awe –
Thy mighty grasp of me.

Out of that weak, unquiet drift
That comes but to depart,
To that pure heaven my spirit lift
Where Thou unchanging art.
Lay hold of me with Thy strong grasp,
Let Thy almighty arm
In its embrace my weakness clasp,
And I shall fear no harm.

Thy purpose of eternal good
Let me but surely know;
On this I'll lean – let changing mood
And feeling come or go –
Glad when Thy sunshine fills my soul,
Not lorn when clouds o'ercast,
Since Thou within Thy sure control
Of love dost hold me fast.

This is the awareness of an existence anchored in its source of the unchanging love of the God Who has created all things in their immensities and in their intensities. In this awareness, time takes on a different context and we are seen no longer as accidents of history, buffeted by fate and chance. Certainly history and what appears to be fate and chance are there. But they too take on a different perspective when that which holds all time is reached to, or rather, when it is perceived that time and its apparent vicissitudes is grasped by that which gave it birth and direction and fulfilment.

Nowhere is the contingency of time, and therefore of our existence in time, so poignantly and comprehensively expressed than in the Psalms. The flesh and blood and human feeling is all there, as it is in the whole necessary epic of Israel recounted in the uniquely Israelitic way throughout the Old Testament. There, the reality of this time of ours and our existence within it, is seen in relational terms. That reality is only such because it is profoundly bracketed in the integrity of its own dimension, with the 'eternity' of God, God's 'time', and therefore God's existence and action.

That reality's full significance is seen in taking stock both of its created nature and identity, and its dependence on its Creator

Who, while standing over and above and beyond it, is nevertheless, in the freedom which He 'eternally' is, committed to be the
God of creation, the Lord of time.

In this dependence alone can it have its own integrity, and in
the light of that dependence alone can its integrity be appreciated.

In his various voices throughout the history of Israel, the
Psalmist expresses this:

> In Thy Light we see light[6]
>
> My time is secure in Thy hands.[7]

He is also aware of the reality of time as it appears to us, and
cries out of that realization.

> So teach us to number our days that we may get us an heart of
> wisdom;[8]
>
> Lord, make me to know mine end, and the measure of my days,
> what it is: that I may know how frail I am.[9]
>
> And now, Lord, what do I wait for? My hope is in Thee.[10]

The Psalms, out of the flesh and blood realities of Israel's
circumstances, are a veritable treasure house of expressions of the
human crying after that which seeks rationality in all the ebb and
flow of human experiences. As such, they are collectively a
striving after an understanding of our existence as contingent
from the God Who has given us identity and dimension, space
and time, and contingent to the God on Whom all this depends.

These voices heard whisperingly in the matrix out of which the
Creator became one of his own creatures, and joined the contingency
from God with the contingency *to* God, born as he was out of the
womb of Israel, are the birth right of the Word made flesh, Jesus
Christ. Here, in Him, intensely alone and immensely operative, time
and our existence characterized 'in' time, is gathered up and given a
context. The great issue between God and humanity is wrought out.

Theology is essentially Christology. Otherwise it is lifeless
deism and stultified rationalism, only another quirk adding to the
confusion of our understanding and, in Kierkegaardian terms,
reducing itself to an insubstantial phenomenon incapable of
wounding what it ought to attack, or healing that which it ought
to bind up.

Theology, as basically and formatively Christology, can point
here to the Person and Event of Jesus Christ unashamedly. It
must, no, it *may*, say:

'This is the point where we stand. From it we converse with all who are concerned with disciplined thought about the truth of our existence, who appreciate the necessary awe and reverence we must have as the realities of time and space unfold themselves to our respectful faithful endeavours in our several explorations.

'This is the ground on which we stand. Let us, from our vantage point call to you and inform you of what we see, and you, from your place of vision, call out to us. Do not dismiss us as putting our trust in unproven things, as if we were advocating the supposed compensating harmonies of a world to come, a nebulous heaven, to divert attention from what we have to cope with here. It is in the "here", in the little things, as well as in the vast things, that we see God's hands and involvement. The Creator Who determined a beginning and therefore, if He is a God of order and precision and faithfulness, a reason and a destiny, works both in the vastness of the universe and in the seemingly insignificant. You know the importance of the little in conjunction with the great – the way of the constituents of the smallest particle of matter as parallel to, and bound up with, the immeasurable reaches of space.

'So too God. As Bishop Lancelot Andrewes[11] reminds us, He called Moses, the great lawgiver, out of a cradle of bullrushes, David, the founder of Israel's monarchy out of the sheepfolds, Goliath the tyrant is slain with a pebble, and the Creator of the world is born in a stable, laid in a manger, in little Bethlehem a poor sorry village scarce worth a mention in the midst of the epic of the world and the contemporary might that was Rome, the glory that was Greece, the wealth that was Egypt. A mighty oak from a little acorn; a spreading tree from a grain of mustard seed. The Creator of all as one of His own creatures. The Word, scarcely able to utter a word.

'This is where we stand and the place and time from which we speak. By this microcosm which is Christ, the universe of time is contained. In Thy light we see light – here is the light which lighteneth every one who comes into the world, and here is the well of life, life itself.'

THEOLOGICAL LANGUAGE ABOUT TIME

Theological science and natural science both operate within the same sphere – this world of time and things in which we live and move and have our being as rational and communicating creatures of, and bounded by, that dimension. They each pursue their respective ends with methods appropriate to the realities which are the objects of their study. The nature of these realities dictate the way in which both sciences distinctively think and speak. Their thought forms and terminology are formed under compulsion of these objective realities so that ways of thinking and speaking are made appropriate to the nature of these realities. Mental endeavour and language become seemly in the company of these objectivities, and corresponding to their dignities.

Because both theological science and natural science share a common ground, the realities of which overlap in their respective enquiries, where they operate and by which they are limited, that is, the constricts of space and time, they cannot insulate themselves from each other. Theology speaks first of God and then, in that controlling context, of God's creation. Natural science explores the realities of that creation from within, as it were, reaching to its boundaries as the dimension of created verities unfolds itself to the mind respectful of it. This common ground means that there must be a concourse and a conversation between the two, because questions are raised by each and posed to the other. The subject of light is an example of this shared concern. This mutual questioning has the beneficial effect of safeguarding against the intrusion of unwarranted presuppositions and subjective ways of thinking on both sides. The procedures of enquiry, the improvement of ways of serving the objective realities which are the scope of each science and the methods of articulating resulting knowledge, can be sharpened and deepened by the correct and respectful use of analogies and modes of thought taken from the other science, particularly when areas of enquiry overlap.

Four things must be borne in mind here:

First, that if knowledge is to be more than mere personal opinion, the authority by which that knowledge is gleaned must reside in the object of which knowledge is desired. If authority were to be transferred to the thinking subject's mind, we could force our own interpretations upon the object and construe it and interpret it as we will.

Second, it follows that there must be an intellectual 'repentance' of the mind. For if the mind is to receive such knowledge, it must deny its own presuppositions and inclinations and reject the temptation to impose them upon the objective realities of its study. The mind has to bow in obedience to the demands of what an object is in itself as it confronts the mind, if we are to come to a full appreciation of its objective reality. It must allow authority to be transferred to the objective reality and away from its own habitual processes of thought. Only as it does so can the mind be rationally obedient and allow reality to reveal itself in its intrinsic objectivity. The mind then is the dutiful servant of reality and not the master of it.

Third, even having done that, caution must be exercised that the truths about a particular sphere of objective reality are not set down in a once and for all system. The pre-eminence always belongs to the objective reality. It was what it is before we began thinking about it. And what it is in itself is that which has made us think about it in a particular way, for it itself forms our thoughts. These thoughts have always to be held secondary to the objective reality which must always remain primary. The danger of a system is that it subtly assumes the primacy and petrifies knowledge, and authority is transferred away from intrinsic objectivity and given to laws and observations which may be deduced out of that system. All thoughts and observations have to be referred to, and tested against, again and again, the compelling objectivity of whatever object forms the field of study. The mind and its 'conclusions' have to undergo a process of constant reformation against the standards of intrinsic reality.

Fourth, it follows that we must distinguish between truth itself and our statements about truth. This is especially so in the question of the Self-revelation of God in Jesus Christ. There God gives himself to be known, but does not thereby give himself up. Although he accommodates himself to this created dimension and to the limitations of humanity and human thought within it, he remains God and Lord over our thoughts. He may be comprehended by us in Jesus Christ, but we comprehend him as Lord and God, and therefore cannot apprehend him. But this is also true of objects within the created dimension. The necessary awe and humility, of which Einstein spoke, which we ought to have in face of the marvellous rationality intrinsic in all levels of created reality, is a general rule of approach to and continuance in study.

These four points are matters internal to each area of discipline. But they are safeguarded by cross-reference with other disciplines, that we may learn from the efforts of others looking at the same field of enquiry in terms of rational objectivity but from different angles, as it were. Again, light is a case in point – and light is integrally bound up with the question of the nature of Time. Theological statement about uncreated light and created light, the rationality of God and the corresponding rationality of the created dimension, have much to learn from, and much to offer to, the observations of pure physics made from a different angle. In this interchange, subjectivism and artificial systemisation are guarded against, and the enquiring mind forced back to activity in accordance with that objective rationality which is truth itself.

If theology were to be regarded as an exercise undertaken in isolation from all other spheres of the endeavour of the human intellect and activity, this would produce a two-fold effect. It would first mean that we were speaking of a God Who had no contact – or at the best a most tenuous relation – with the realities which surround us and of which we are part. We would have immediately entered into a dualism, where the only contact with God was through the human imagination or by way of so-called spiritual exercises. This disjunction of God from the world of time and things and the degeneration of theology into a superficial mysticism, severs the proper ground of being of all things from the things themselves. There is no idea of a profound relationship between Creator and creature, and therefore the full significance of the created realities are not spoken of or addressed. Theology becomes superfluous and meaningless, for it has nothing to say to life in the midst of the realities of this world of time and space – indeed its true but sometimes hidden purpose is to escape them. In this fundamental questions have to be asked as to what such a theology is saying about human existence. For that existence is bound, by its very nature, to this sphere of time and things. Is it in fact denying the very nature of humanity and positing a gnostic anthropology?

Secondly, an isolated theology produces language about God at a tangent. It can only speak of God in mythological terms, for while it seeks to escape the limitations of space and time, it only has a language formed by the restrictions of space and time, and must therefore bend these terms to suit that which is beyond and which has nothing in common with the created realities, or invent a new terminology. Theological language and terminology becomes aesthetic, detached and merely oblique. It becomes esoteric, known only to the initiate, for the justification of such terminology is only derived from a supposed religious consciousness or imagination. It is purely subjective. God becomes a product of the individual religious self-consciousness. So much of what is called 'spiritual' – that over-worked and rarely defined term covering much that is nebulously subjective – has its inception here.

This is not to say, however, that all theological language must be immediate and conclusive. That is to fall into another error, that of literalism or fundamentalism, in which Truth is confused with statements about Truth, and Truth circumscribed by the limitations of human thought.

Theological language will be neither of these, neither tangential nor literal. It will be paradeigmatic, that is, of the nature of pointing beyond itself obedient to the nature of that about which it is speaking. In a sense, theological language is parabolic. It speaks in parables about that which can only appear to us as Parable, God as the essential Parable of all. God's Self-disclosure in Jesus Christ, the Revelation of himself in our humanity in all his Godness, still is that Parable, for that can never be subsumed by the human intellect and explained away. It confront us as 'the mystery of Godliness' (that is, 'Godness').

But if theology is either tangential or literal, then Christianity is turned into a religion – an endeavour of man the individual. Christian practice is transformed into religiosity – the scruple of the like-minded initiates. 'Religion' is certainly related to 'religare', 'to tie' or 'to bind', here.

The converse to this is that if theology becomes so anchored in the concerns of the created realities that it cannot raise its head to perceive that which gives them reality and identity, this too produces a two-fold effect. First it would mean that we were speaking of a God Who had no existence apart from the world. God is perceived as the highest or best expression of what we already know and experience. We would have entered into a confusion, where immediate contact with God was via participation in political, social or cultural enterprises. This qualitative confusion of God with the values and norms of humanity – and, indeed, with the beauties of nature – deifies that which we already know and perceive and practise. There is no idea of the God Who is the source and bestower of being and order and Who is Order and Being himself, to Whom all things have to be referred for an appreciation of their context and therefore their true significance. It cannot speak of anything greater than this sphere we know, and its activity is wasted within its relativities. Such theology is ultimately discredited because it cannot raise the hopes of any field of endeavour or activity above the transitoriness and relativities of this dimension of time and things. Nor can it be the matrix from which great endeavours and achievements come forth.

Secondly, such theology employs a language which is no different in the content of its terminology from the common usage around it. The tendency here is to transfer the ordinary content of imagery with its everyday understanding of that usage and meaning, to the God of Whom it speaks. God, therefore, is not greater than the bounds of our ability, and becomes but a projection of social conscience, political allegiance or cultural awareness.

Christianity is also here turned into a religion – an endeavour of collective man. Christian practice is transformed into religiosity – the deification of a particular politico-social and cultural activism. Here too it is tied and bound to manifestos dictated by other considerations.

It them becomes stuck, for its proclamation is but that which is known already from other sources and accepted from current fashion – or it drifts into the next cultural instalment but always after the criteria of acceptance have already become fixed by other cultural forces. In either case it has nothing to say in the last resort.

The necessity of objective thought stands at the head of every theological endeavour. This is not to say that the subjective is dismissed out of hand and absolutely. In any theological activity, the existence of the thinking subject has to be borne in mind. His or her experiences may have much to do with throwing light on their findings – either by way of perceiving original thought or confirming prejudices. The problem is that the subjective has to be placed, with due accord, in its relationship to that which is primary, namely, the acknowledgement that truth exists and will exist as it is in itself whatever may be said about it.

But when we consider the problem of Time, and what path theology is to take in such a consideration, we must be aware – and beware – of very strong subjective elements which cannot be discarded, but which have to be placed in their proper context.

So compelling are these subjectivities that some of them could be reduced to a type of solipsism, the lurking impression that time only exists for me, or slightly better, that time is only what I feel it to be. They are compelling because of the particular way in which existence is bound up with time, not only for duration but in matters of quality of life. A span of time as measured by the clock, for example could be to one individual the proverbial 'eternity' of waiting and suspense, while the same measure for another person could, in his enjoyment, be a matter of 'time flying'. And as for the reality of that 'span' of time – if there were no clock would it have duration, and, if so, by what is it objectively measured? By the movement of heavenly bodies? But if there were no heavenly bodies . . .? The problem which arises here is the relation of things, or existence, to time. If nothing existed, would there still be such an entity as time? Or is Time indissolubly bound with existence? The cynic might say that if there were no existence there would be no one to think about time anyway, so what is the point? But this does highlight the difficulty of the question of Time's objectivity.

This is but a superficial comment – yet a very real one – on the problem of the relation of the objective and the subjective in the matter of Time.

There is indeed another problem fast on the heels of this. This was highlighted in J. W. Dunne's book *An Experiment with Time*.[12] If I think about Time, it takes me time to so think. So while I consider one layer of Time, there is, so to speak, another layer behind this, a Time about Time. Here, too, the subjective and the objective are embroiled. For in thinking at all, I have to think about thinking; I have to look at myself and examine my ways. Parallel therefore to a Time beside Time (which Dunne calls 'serial' time and points out that thought can suggest a whole series of such series) there is the astonishing possibility which thought can produce that there is a 'serial me'. For each thinking observer there has to be another layer of thought which means in effect stepping outside ourselves to take a look at ourselves. But the very process of so doing requires a farther step and a farther ad infinitum!

This line of argument, says Dunne, can only lead to perplexing 'three-dimensional instabilities', for his thesis is that wholeness and completion of thought on such matters, and the nature of Time itself in its series, can only be resolved when four dimensional contexts are realized. These contexts are not clear to the observer because he constantly reverts to thinking in terms of three-dimensional perplexities.

Whatever the validity of Dunne's argument, and whether or not his 'four-dimensional' theories hold (and indeed if any of his theories, now presumably dated, hold – the Damoclean judgement on anyone who would write about time!), this is a theological exercise and it is not within the brief of our consideration to begin with his premises. Such should be noted and particularly the observations of natural science as it presently has developed, listened to and regarded. But the reference to Dunne's work serves to warn about the complexity of thinking about Time, the scope of such an endeavour, and the absurdities which lie in wait.

Where then may the theologian, while bearing in mind the enquiries of other branches of science, begin to make an entrance into the objective aspect of time? Where is this primacy of objectivity to be sought? And what place is to be accorded to the subjective?

We approach this in the first instance by stating what may be the obvious; our difficulty in speaking about Time.

This difficulty is two-fold.

First, there is the necessity of theologically looking at Time and applying rationally a theological method in this particular sphere.

Second there is the necessity of finding theological terms appropriate to the nature of Time.

But if faced with trying to see if there is an objectivity of Time, how can we address these two necessities? By what standard is our method and terminology deemed appropriate? We have not even begun to discover the means of measuring propriety. In this we must be supremely honest in order to avoid an imbalance of subjectivism.

The insurmountable difficulty in writing about time is that we are faced with attempting to describe the indescribable. The reason for this is that we just do not have the vocabulary to cope with it. Our language and thought are forged within the temporal dimension; we cannot stand outside time and discover a terminology suitable for an analysis and description of time itself.

We are faced, therefore with the dilemma of employing what are necessarily static terms to deal with what is elusively dynamic and beyond the boundaries of our comprehension. This was the limitation of Isaac Newton, that, magnificent and far-reaching as his achievement was, absolute time and space were reduced to a rigid framework of mathematical turgidity.

On the simplest level this language difficulty is demonstrated by the necessity of employing temporal terms to speak of eternity: 'before time was'. This leads, if such language is taken literally, to the assumption that there is time before time and that therefore eternity is endless time. Alternatively, that which is beyond time is described as 'timelessness' – a totally unmeaningful term, which presupposes that time exists in an independent isolation.

The language used about time may have to be seen as parabolic. That is, perhaps we can only talk about it in parables, enigmas, paradeigmatically. Our terminology must then point beyond itself to what cannot be encompassed within it. It will be seen to be directional rather than conclusive, provisional rather than final. St Paul's 'we see through a glass darkly . . . but then face to face', referring to our estate and circumstances here compared with the 'then' of the fulfilment of all things, is apposite here.

However, the very process of attempting to find directional terms and thought forms which are precise, so that clarity of direction is presented, may of itself have much to say about the nature and use of theological language. Such endeavours can only be ventured upon with a constant and discerning eye to the nature of language appropriate to what is being studied. For any reality studied unfolds itself as it allows us to penetrate its nature, provided that we do no violence to it by imposing upon it our subjective presuppositions. Propriety of terms and thought forms is itself then created and clarified under the compulsive objectivity of that reality revealing itself before us.

It is the fact that we experience time which causes the difficulty. Nowhere does subjectivism run so deeply as in the matter of time. 'My time', 'our time'; such phrases betray the idea that we possess time. This is coloured by either an attempted mastery of the question of time for us (clairvoyancy, fortune-telling, astrology) or an unconscious feeling of its mastery over us (that form of paramnesia which is the sense of deja-vu, the feeling that time goes in joys quickly, in troubles slowly, the ever-present shadow of things left undone or done wrongly). Our feelings and time are indissoluble.

Hence the problem of extricating ourselves from our subjective views about time. Yet there is a necessary link between existence, experience and time. We are creatures who live and move and have their being 'in' time. Time, it is commonly said, takes its toll upon us. We are born, grow up, grow old and die, some sooner, some later. We may live with hopes or fears – that is with expectations or anxieties about the future, some imaginary, some all too real. But die we must and so inevitably become part of the past, some remembered, some forgotten. Our existence is inextricably interwoven with time; it is determined by it.

The problem of acknowledging this relation between time and our existence, and striking a balance between a necessarily objective view of time while recognising our particular, necessary subjective implication in it, leads to a more general consideration which is the next difficulty encountered.

This is the fact that time is not itself an independent 'thing'. Theologically speaking it is 'co-created'. There is no Biblical notion of time being created as a thing in itself. Time begins with the creation of things, that is space or place. It happens to be because of the dimension and nature of space. It happens secondarily although as a necessary corollary to creation.

How then can we be objective about something which has no independent existence or significance? Are we forced into a view that subjectivism must reign supreme, and capitulate to the idea that time is what everybody makes it for himself or herself? Is the fact of time what everybody makes it to be? Does its reality consist of mere subjective experience, and therefore it has as many 'realities' as there are individuals?

It is clear that there is a common existence shared by all individuals. All are related to time within certain given parameters, namely their conception, birth and death. To that extent, time is more than the individual. Its giveness is shared by all; its quality for each of them another matter. But these events concerning every individual presuppose a possible movement of time. On the other hand, it is an equal possibility that time stands still and the individuals move within its static state. Is time in a state of continual equilibrium? Certainly individuals more towards what might be called their final equilibrium, death itself. But is this a movement of time along with which they are borne?

This is a third major difficulty; this question of the movement of time. Strangely there is no scientific proof for the direction of time's possible movement. The principles deduced from the present theory of general relativity, for example, would still hold good if time moved backwards. Nor are the various findings from quantum theory as they now stand of any help.

The authors of *The Arrow of Time* point out that in the fundamental question of the direction of time, there is silence in these quarters. Both quantum mechanics and relativity, in their present formulation, are reversible, and of no help in the question.

Thermodynamics, according to these authors, comes to the rescue[13]. The irreversible direction of time is indicated strongly by the irreversible loss of heat from any object. A heated object will loose heat until it reaches a stage of equilibrium, that is, a temperature equal to that of its surroundings. This loss in all ways is common to all things. Decay of age is the most obvious example. Entropy, the measure of the capacity to change, is inseparably linked with time. (It must not be thought however, that the Second Law of Thermodynamics claims a uniform degeneration of all things into random chaos). Apart from this, it may be claimed by many that it is a matter of common sense that time flows in one direction – a direction which is commonly split into past, present and future, wherein the past is fixed as that which has gone and the future that which is to come.

But in this proposition of the irreversible movement of time, what do we mean by 'past, present and future'. How are they to be defined? What constitutes them? Our fourth major difficulty is finding a vantage point from which to view these supposed categories in this supposed direction of time. 'There is no time like the present' may well be that which is advised by this vaunted common sense. But what is the present? It is indefinable. Even in the pronunciation of the word 'now', short as it is, the first sound on the initial consonant has gone into the past before that sound is completed. 'Now' has no place. The present would have to be regarded as the meeting point of future with past, rather as a tangent touches a circle, that is touches it but without measurement. In other words the use of the word 'present' merely indicates a convenient way of describing that flux in which the mind is both a memory still vivid for the immediate past and an open anticipation for that which is to come immediately (it may not, of course!). The problem of the present eludes resolution into a description of a quantifiable and observable state. The present can be no vantage point.

This is a theological study. Therefore, certain conditions are laid down, bearing in mind the observations above about the necessity of terminology being appropriate to the nature of the object studied. To look at time, or indeed any thing else, theologically means that we have to begin where theology begins. On that basis we look at time, but with recourse to what other disciplines say about time, so that parallels in thought and refinement of terminology might be appreciated to mutual benefit in the question of the mystery of time. It will, in all probability remain a mystery both for theologians and natural scientists. Roger Penrose of Oxford may well be right in thinking that the understanding of physical reality, as we conceive it at present, especially concerning our attitudes towards the nature of time, requires a radical reform, even more so than the revolution which has been provided by the development of relativity and quantum mechanics.

Whether such a 'shake-up' would resolve the question of time is another matter. It would lead undoubtedly to furtherance of understanding. The theologian can only say that any creature can only be understood in the light of the Creator, and that this includes the question of time. It also includes the theological fact that 'then' (that is when time is fulfilled in the decree of God) 'we shall know'. The entrance into the theological task takes stock of the Apostle's following words 'even as we now are known'.

It is there that we begin.

I

Theological Questions about Time

KARL BARTH, at the beginning of his section on 'The Time of Revelation' in *Church Dogmatics*,[1] asserts that the statement 'God reveals Himself' is a statement about an event and the time proper to this event. It is therefore synonymous with 'God has time for us'. Barth begins an interpretation of this 'revelation time' by claiming that it is to be understood only on the basis of what revelation is, and therefore how that time is determined and qualified. To attempt an understanding of it from the point of view of a concept of time gained from any other source or consideration, is to fit revelation and the nature of the time of this event into an alien and presupposed framework. In such an attempt, God's revelation of himself, the time he has for us, is thereby subordinated to the authority of supposed anterior and superior factors. But this revelation as an event is self-declaratory as to its quality and its time.

Underlying and underpinning such an assertion is Barth's fidelity to the orthodox position of, among others, Irenaeus and Athanasius in their respective generations. This emphasis states that God comes to us on his own terms; that he is his own interpreter; that only by God can God be known;[2] that there is no disjunction between the being of God and his acts; that knowledge of God as revealed in Christ is not disinterested information or static propositions about a static object, but a sharing in the knowledge which God has of himself in his Triune existence;[3] that what he is eternally in himself he is towards us in Jesus Christ.[4]

It is also part of Barth's own insistence that there is no Natural Theology apart from and in addition to the revelation of God in Christ. There is, therefore, no authority other than Christ in his Self-disclosure as the Self-revelation of God, by which an understanding of him and the things pertaining to this Christ-event (and in this case the time of revelation) can be reached. Only within the light and terms of Revealed Theology is a true Natural Theology to be found. Indeed, all of Barth's observations on Natural Theology and therefore his stance concerning grounds of supposed authority as preconditions for theological thinking and investigation other than that revelation, are but an extended commentary on these Patristic dicta.[5] It is all very much a case of 'In thy light we see light', or, with this matter, In thy time we see time.

There are, according to Barth,[6] three categories of time; God-created time, our time, and the time of God's revelation.

That time which God brought into being at creation is now hidden and withdrawn from us, for the Fall intervenes between that created time and our time.

Our time is lost time, fallen time. On the basis of the time of revelation and what is revealed to us in that time, we may perceive that God is the Creator of all and has created what we call time, but we also must acknowledge that there is a qualitive difference between our time, the time we know which is character-ised by our estate, and that first, God-created time.

Barth then points out that if God's revelation has a time, the time of the event of Jesus Christ, the time which God has for us in our fallen estate and time, it must be a third time alongside God-created time and our time. These last two cannot be under-stood out of themselves. Just how impossibly elusive God-created time is, and just how problematic it is to try to understand our time out of itself, is illustrated by three difficulties. Any concept of time, wherever gleaned, has to face these.

Before Barth's outlining of three difficulties in the formulation of any idea of time are set out, we have to take stock of the use by theologians of another concept, that of 'eternity'. Of itself, and probably as popularly used, 'eternity' can be regarded as a meaningless term. However, we ask here that it be accepted, albeit only as an assumption, with the following meaning: that the concept of 'eternity' is a theological category to express that which is 'beyond', 'over' and 'above' time. It refers in the first and determinative instance, to God himself. There is no eternity apart from God. If there were such a 'dimension' which God happened to inhabit, it would have pre-eminence over him. It is because there is an eternal God that there is an eternity, which may be defined as the 'time' and 'place' of God as compared with our time and place within the created dimension. Barth's warnings about difficulties in thinking about time are set out in this way:

1. What is the present? The present is the fulcrum of past and

future. It is the point (to use a concept which has to be developed, but which is a convenience used at this stage of the unfolding and unravelling, and teasing out of the strands of the argument) from which past is recollected and future hopes emerge. It is so *fleeting* that as soon as one syllable is written or spoken, the past is already past and the future there. But what is this point? Is it tangible? Does it have existence and is it a third thing together with the past and future. Is it indeed, (here Barth notes Augustine's assertion on the matter) an original thing? But these very questions as to the nature of the present show our perplexity about time itself.

2. Despite appearances to the contrary, does time have a beginning and an end, or is it without such? Does a beginning of time imply the end of a past time, so that there is a series of times with beginnings and ends? But such a serial still says nothing about time itself. Does the present have anything to say about the nature of time regarding a possible beginning and ending? If there is a beginning and an end, the present, as Augustine saw,[7] would have to move forward so that the past increases in quantity and the future decreases. But if time were endless, without beginning and end, this move forward would be an illusion and the present in fact stationary. At what point would it be stationary, and if it were, how would the past be recognized as the past and the future as the future? So again we have a perplexity about time which we cannot resolve.

3. What is the relation between time and eternity? Does eternity stand at the boundaries of time, at its possible beginning and end? In which case eternity stands in a loose conjunction with time, remote enough to have nothing to say about the nature of time save that it is that from which escape may be made into eternity. Or is there such a union between time and eternity that time is to be seen as the vessel of eternity so that every moment has an eternal significance? It is of little use if we seek to avoid the question of the objectivity of time as an entity in any relation to eternity and pose the question subjectively, namely: do I come from eternity and go to meet it, or do I already have eternity? Yet again there seems to be no satisfactory answer in all these questions to give us any confidence as to our ability to cope with the nature of time.

Barth's position is that we cannot speak of time on the grounds of 'God-created' time or 'our' time. These insurmountable questions will continually intrude in our supposed solutions to the problem. The theologian can only speak of time on the basis of the third category, that is, the time which God has for us in revelation, in Jesus Christ. It is here that eternity is in perfect union with time, and a vantage point therefore given. For in becoming flesh and entering the realities of 'our' time, 'fallen' time, God remains what he eternally is. The Word was made flesh, time is given existence in union with the Eternal. Here we have an entrance into the question of time, for it opens out to us in its context, its relation to the One by whom all things (and therefore what we call 'time') were created.

The theologian's claim is that time and eternity possess a unique relation here in the time of revelation because of the taking up of the creature into union with the Creator at the Incarnation of the Eternal Word or Son of God.

We have to point out that there are two distinct approaches in the development of Barth's thought. Throughout his *Church Dogmatics*, Barth makes constant excuse for the position he had adopted previously in his *Commentary on the Epistle to the Romans* – but with reservations as if he was still pondering on its lasting value. This is the later 'dialogical' Barth looking with some askance at his previous 'dialetical' self – even if he disliked these labels. Nevertheless, we note that former position of Barth, for it has an approach which has to be considered even if only for a clarifying of our own approach to the question of time.

In that *Commentary on the Epistle to the Romans*, he had written[8] of the significance of the phrase 'Jesus Christ our Lord'. This, says Barth, is the Gospel and the meaning of history (and therefore of time). But this is expressed in terms of tension and crisis between that which is known and that which is unknown.

> In this name two worlds meet and go apart, two planes inter-
> sect, the one known and the other unknown. The known plane
> is God's creation, fallen out of its union with Him, and there-
> fore the world of the 'flesh' needing redemption, the world of
> men, and of time, and of things – our world. This known plane
> is intersected by another plane that is unknown – the world of
> the Father, of the Primal Creation, and of the final
> Redemption.

In the declaration (which is beyond historical definition and comprehension) that Jesus Christ is the Son of God in the Resurrection, we affirm that we can only deal with him as the

End of History . . . as Paradox (Kierkegaard), as Victor (Blum-
hardt), as Primal History (Overbeck).

The Resurrection is the *declaration* of this world of the Father
of which we, in time, can know nothing. The Resurrection is the
establishing of

the new world of the Holy Spirit.

In the Resurrection, this new world

touches the old world of the flesh, but touches it as a tangent
touches a circle, that is, without touching it. And, precisely
because it does not touch it, it touches it as its frontier – as the
new world. The Resurrection is therefore an occurence in history,
which took place outside the gates of Jerusalem in the year AD
30, inasmuch as it there 'came to pass', was discovered and
recognized. But inasmuch as the occurrence was conditioned by
the Resurrection, in so far, that is, as it was not the 'coming to
pass' or the discovery, or the recognition, which conditioned its
necessity and appearance and revelation, the Resurrection is not
an event in history at all:

This last comment – 'not an event in history at all' – requires
some elucidation. If this whole argument is applied to time – an
application entirely permissible on Barth's own terms, as the
event of revelation has its own self-authenticated time – then
something profound is being asked in a way not previously
entered upon, about the nature of time.

Even for the dialectic Barth, with all his language of crisis,
judgment and negation, this revelation occurrence of resurrection
is nevertheless related to all history, though it is 'not an event in
history at all'. For it is precisely on the basis of crisis, judgment,
negation and 'otherness', that time is established in a positive
relationship with eternity. All false views and expectations concerning time are cleared and the decree of God for all time seen.

The years AD 1–3 are the era of revelation and disclosure; the era
which . . . sets forth the new and strange and divine definition of
all time. The particularity of the years AD 1–30 is dissolved by
this divine definition, because it makes every epoch a potential
field of revelation and disclosure.

The argument which Barth develops about this relation is that
old time and the old world is but a 'no' to the truth of the new

time and the new world. The very relationship highlights the distinction – which means that all things (and all time) are held in tension and crisis.

> But these two worlds do not exist side by side, nor do the old and new man compose two men. For the possibility of the one involves the impossibility of the other; and the impossibility of the one involves the possibility of the other. Regarded from the point of view of the 'first' world, the 'second' ceases to be a second: and from the point of view of the 'second', the 'first' ceases to be a first. What is non-existent in the first world forms the very existence of the second; and what constitutes the existence of the first is non-existent in the second.

It is this factor of tension and crisis and otherness in the relation between time and eternity which Barth has perhaps too quickly dismissed in his later thought. He does say in *Church Dogmatics* that such views of the crisis between time and eternity, Creator and creature, might have been right for that time in European history and the then state of theology when he wrote his *Commentary on Romans*. He saw that particular age and culture and the role which theology played then, as a time when radical questions had to be posed in order to bring theology back to fundamentals and out of the romanticism and subjectivism by which it had become indistinguishable from cultural views and opinions.

But there is still this question of what is meant by 'a point' – the tangential meeting place of eternity in time. It may be noted that he has not carried this concept of crisis into his later theological thought about time and eternity, but masked the necessary radicalism of that point where time and eternity are related in the way in which he expresses it, to the detriment of the full extent of its implications.

This expression is found fully in *Church Dogmatics*, Vol. III:2, pp. 457–640, and we will distill and comment on certain sections as a development of what has been said so far.

The time of Jesus Christ, that is from his conception to his Resurrection, is the fulfilment of all time. Time itself, from its beginning to its end, is enfolded or recapitulated in him. All things, including time which is the necessary by-product of created space, are related to him. For the moment we express this in a two-fold way, though later we will wish to modify this and express a more radical interpretation of it.

All things, including time, are related to Jesus Christ by virtue of his Divinity; he is the One by Whom all things were and are created. All things, including time, are related to him by virtue of his Incarnation; while remaining God without laying aside, compromising or diluting the reality of his eternal Godness, He takes the reality of this created order, including time, to himself in inseparable but unconfused union. The Creator becomes one of his own creatures. The Word becomes a child unable to utter a word. The Eternal takes temporality to himself.

But the time of this man, gathering up all time in his day, is unique. Such cannot be postulated of any other human being. For no other human being is God or in relation to God in this way by virtue of their humanity having existence only in union with the Eternal Word. It is the relation of the humanity to the Divinity which is the principle of the gathering up of all things. It is as the Word made flesh that the man Jesus is the Lord of time, embracing and affecting time from its beginning to its end. Time past and time future is gathered up as present to his time. As the Lord of time he is the fulfilment of time.

For all others in their time, time is a vastly different matter. We are far from being lords of time. If anything, to take a cursory glance at the matter, we appear rather as prisoners of time, held by its relentless march. We once had a time, our past, which is ours no longer – nor can we do anything about it. We have a history, written and unalterable. We may have a time, our future, which is not yet ours – nor can we count on it. If we have a future it can only be one of tenuous hope. In this cursory glance, time is our master both in the severity of our past and the elusiveness of our future.

We have left our past, we are in it no more. It cannot be recalled and the things done undone, and the things not done accomplished. Nothing can be restored; it has all passed us by into what is mainly oblivion.

That blankness is relieved somewhat, but only partially (and that highly selective) by memory. Faces, names, happenings and surroundings may appear in shadow in the memory, some vague and wraithlike, some clear and well-defined. We must not forget that most of our life is made up of memories, although to be absorbed merely or even chiefly in memory is a sign either of old age or of reluctance to accept whatever may surround us. Memory is the subjective skill with which we seek to be present in the past, but it has no objective ability to allow us to relive that which is gone.

Equally we must not forget the blessed gift of forgetfulness! There is undoubtedly a happy oblivion in which past unfortunate circumstances, sorrows, regretfulness and shame loose their ability to be our present and constant companions. If they are such, then that is a sign of a deep disorder by which the past exercises a psychological tyranny over us.

Both memory and oblivion emphasise the gulf which lies between us and our past time. We no longer are the people we were years ago, weeks ago, even seconds ago. We may wish to adhere to the past, but we press on while the unreturnable past slips away from us as the flow of a stream. The future calls us and invites us.

Similarly the future is separated from us. It is possible to recall something of the past in memory, even if insubstantially. It is not possible (even for the highly dubious activity of clairvoyancy) to grasp the future and know some substantiality of coming events before they happen, if happen they will. We do not even know if we have a future, a time to come which will be our time, just as the past was our past. We may, of course, have expectations and hopes, anxieties and fears, intentions and schemes, but this is the only way in which we can approach the future.

The future may be anticipated in cheerfulness – 'the future looks rosy', 'we will do this', 'we will do that'. In this way we approach the future optimistically, but in mere anticipation. The very phrase 'looking forward to . . .' has almost an element of impudent assumption challenging the future. But challenge implies combat, and we cannot foresee by what terms that will be waged. But at least we encourage ourselves and in a sense arm ourselves in this way, even if it is with sticks against iron.

The future may be anticipated in fear – 'what will we do if . . .?' In this way we approach the future dismally, but, again, in mere anticipation. Pessimism is not necessarily prudence, however, nor is it indisputably preparedness – we can be in danger of tilting at windmills in the mind and diverting our attention from a more seemly attitude of patient hope.

So insubstantial and unforeseeable is the future that we tend to want to fill it prematurely with our own devices, thus avoiding the true nature of that which eludes us. There is nothing definite in these, and we seem to have an instinctive awareness of this, surrounding ourselves, as we do, with pithy and proverbial sayings in the matter – 'tempting providence', 'chancing fate', 'counting chickens before they are hatched'. The best laid plans can go awry, however carefully prepared and laid they may be; the worst expectations, even if based on past experience, not realized. The anticipation and the reality are not necessarily one, the latter quite and usually capable of confounding the former. We tend to be false prophets and impudent soothsayers in this matter.

But the most tantalising obscurity concerning our existence in time is the present. Here we think that we can be assured of who and what we are. We are aware of the present and in this awareness either take our ease and find our security in the identification of ourselves as we really are, or flee from the realization of the persons we are, wishing the time away and hoping for a better future. But what is this awareness of this present? It has in fact no stability or continuance, for the present has no substance or durance. It is but the step between that which no longer is and that which is yet to come. It is the hinge whereby the past opens out to the future.

In this mystery of the present lies the mystery of our existence. Barth is supremely correct in seeing the inseparable connection between time and being. The past can at least be measured; distance lends objectively here at least. It had a continuance and measure of days and years. So too our past being. What happened in the past to us, by us and with us, remembered or forgotten, makes up the measure of what we were in the past, and dictates the sort of person each has come to be. In the same way the future – if it comes – will have a duration of hours and days, and we – if we have a future – will evolve with its circumstances and experiences, and become the persons we will be.

What we were and what we will be balance on this elusive present. Plead as we might that the present may remain and have constancy, it is that which has already gone and has not yet come. We only experienced the present by memories and feelings with regard to the past, and by hopes and fears concerning the future, with the corresponding interpretations of the past and programmes for the future. The present is that infinitesimal point where we exist as what we were and what we will be.

We exist therefore in questionableness, in the inability of doing anything about a past which has eluded us and gone, in the uncertainty of a future which always is a step ahead of us as the 'not yet', and in the fleeting fragility of the present impossible to measure and hold. This 'riddle of time' as Barth describes it, is the enigma of our existence. We may also couple with this the 'three-dimensional absurdities', outlined by the references to J. W. Dunne's work, above.

Here all speculation about time culled from trying to look at time as it appears to us, can only be silenced. Barth draws out the impossibility of such a venture in insisting that we cannot so understand 'our time'. We may also say that it stills and quietens a great deal of nonsense talked about understanding humanity out of itself. Any supposed conclusion on that matter can only find its self-demolition when it takes account of this enigma of time. The test of any anthropological theory is how far it has considered this riddle.

What may be said about this? Have we come to a full stop which indicates the necessary silencing of every voice raised in speculation in this field? We may turn to see what Barth's statement that our time can only be understood in the light of the time of God's Self-revelation has to say on the matter, and whether this establishes guidelines, not necessarily confined to theology. Two considerations may be brought to bear here. The first is *the theological concept of recapitulation* and the second *the theological understanding of parable.*

It is surprising that in this section of Time in his *Church Dogmatics*, Barth does not appeal explicitly to the doctrine of recapitulation, particularly when he is at such pains to interpret our time in the light of the time of the incarnation of the Word by Whom all things were made, the time of Jesus Christ.

Here we may turn to the great exponent in the early Church of the doctrine of recapitulation, St Irenaeus (c. 130–c. 202). The sources for his observations on this subject are: his main extant work, *Adversus Haereses*; *Demonstration of the Apostolic Preaching*, a little handbook of doctrine which has a positive content being a resumé of the larger work but omitting the long explanations of heretical systems which he was encountering; and *Fragments* of lost works. In all these the theme of recapitulations runs as a binding emphasis in all areas of doctrine.

In the brief and general scan of Irenaeus's doctrine of recapitulation and attendant themes which follows, the way in which Barth treats and deals with time as centring on the Incarnation, will be seen to have patristic precedence. While time is not mentioned explicitly in the works of Irenaeus as a doctrine with its own area, it is implicitly contained in the matter of recapitulation.

2

Recapitulation and Time

THE DOCTRINE of Recapitulation figures largely in the works of Irenaeus (c. AD 122–202). Before entering the examination of Irenaeus's main points about recapitulation, and therefore Time, it is necessary to lay out his general theological attitude. Recapitulation – though the same is true of any doctrine – cannot be understood as a doctrine in vacuum. Its implications and breadth are such that it is, in a sense, the sum of all doctrine, or at least, draws from all doctrine. Thus these implications demand an appreciation of the sort of theological terminology in which a particular writer couches the doctrine of recapitulation, and an awareness of how it is approached from that writer's personal angles and emphases.

IRENAEUS AND THEOLOGY: THE NATURE OF THEOLOGICAL STATEMENTS

For Irenaeus, the Faith is *always one and the same*.[1] This does not mean that Christian doctrine has been once and for ever satisfactorily and completely wrapped up in a collection of static statements. On the contrary, doctrine is a lively exercise ever expanding and always expressed in quality of Christian life in particular and all human existence in general. 'Godliness' and 'Truth' are inseparable. It does mean that doctrine (and therefore the quality of Christian life, and, indeed, the fact of human existence *in toto*) are once and for all and unshakeably grounded in the unchangeable reality of the Word made flesh. It is through a *community of union*[2] with Jesus Christ that we are empowered to know God, for this Jesus Christ is God accommodating himself to our limitations. Yet in this self-giving, the eternal Son of God retains as inviolate the mystery of his eternal being which can never be circumscribed by words. God comes to us in Christ on his own terms, and remains Lord over all our thoughts about him. In other words, Irenaeus distinguishes between Truth itself and statements about Truth.

Statements about Truth have constantly to be reformed by

testing them and testing them again against the measure of the objective Truth of God in Christ. Truth itself is always anterior and superior to statements about it, for it is that which calls statements about it into being. In other words, Christ is always Lord even over – or particularly over – our theology.

> ... Faith rests on things that truly are. For in things that are, as they are, we believe; and believing in things that are, as they ever are, we keep firm our confidence in them.[3]

Here we have an assertion of the priority of objective truth over against our subjective perception of it. The truth about anything remains constant, whatever we may say about it. The object of our scrutiny will remain as it is in itself, in its integrity, before we begin thinking about it, as we think about it and after we have thought about it – and despite what we say about it. Our statements about what we perceive to be its actuality have to be distinguished from that truth itself. That truth, in its compelling objectivity, will question our perception of it and call our statements into being as servants of it. Our statements are not lord over it.

Both the Gnostic heretics which Irenaeus countered and the Arian heretics which Athanasius was later to face in the 4th century, did not so distinguish. For them, the truth about something was perfectly capable, provided it was something on the created dimension, of being fully comprehended and contained completely within our thoughts and statements.

Arianism had part of its roots in Gnosticism, and the common ground they shared was that both systems of heresy regarded the eternal Word or Son of God as a creature – the best and first and most glorious of creatures, but nevertheless within the same created dimension as ourselves. Therefore he was open to being fully described by, and contained within, human statements about him.

In this way, both systems projected the nature of creatureliness into God. They blurred the distinction between Creator and creature. They used images and symbols about God not as pointers to him, nor appropriately chosen in the light of God's self-revelation in Christ. The *content* of these images were thus regarded as truths about God. This is why both systems became entangled in terms of human generation as applied to God. 'Father' and 'son' meant from them literally what we mean by these terms as applied to human beings.[4] The ludicrousness of this is apparent, for if such content is projected into God, then, rationally, God must have a wife and a father and so on. The projection of the images of human sexuality into God,[5] led to a paganisation of Christianity.

God infinitely transcends all human terminology and its content. Verbal images employed in thinking and speaking of God must be appropriate, insofar as they can, to the terms of his self-revelation, yet recognize their essential impropriety. This is the constant tension of theology whereby its faithfulness to the object of its scrutiny is a matter of constant endeavour, testing and reformation with regard to its terminology. It is in the proper sense 'dialectic' thinking, for even if theology is construed as dialogical thinking, whereby there is a 'conversation' between object and thinking subject (the object in this case being God in his self-giving and 'speaking' in Jesus Christ) nevertheless this tension must always be to the fore, otherwise a subjective assumption of authority over the object inevitably results, and one type or other of fundamentalism emerges as a theological system.

This lies behind the description of much of the Gnostic systems in *Adversus Haereses* by Irenaeus, particularly when he outlines the heretics' view of the generation of the Son of God, and the questions which they raise and pretend to solve. One such prime question concerns what sphere lies beyond God the Father (that is, 'has God got a greater God beyond him, a God who begat him?'). That such question could be asked (as indeed they are still asked by children in one form or another) is the result of the projection of the temporal dimension and temporal values into God. God is treated as ultimately on the same level as all else, and therefore as lying within the circumscribing and concluding capabilities of the human mind.

Temporal images as 'the hand of God', etc., cannot be literally applied to God. Images are helpful to mankind, but not appropriate to God. Images are only props for the mind to grasp on to in order to raise itself above them. And they have to be appropriate props if we are to be pointed in the right direction. Not only are they but props, but they have to take a shift in meaning from their everyday usage to be appropriate in any measure, for the particular theological meaning they assume is determined by the nature of what they are trying to point to – that is, the revelation of God in Christ.

By ignoring or rejecting this, the heretical systems of Gnosticism and Arianism brought the revelation of God, and so God himself, within the compass and supposed sufficiency of the relativities of language and terminology. Our terminology and images could be imposed upon God instead of, as both Irenaeus and Athanasius in their insistence that God is without comparison[6] emphasise, our language and symbols being chosen and formed and bent out of their everyday use into this particular usage by the impact of that revelation, and made appropriate pointers – pointing beyond their human and created content – to that indescribable mystery of the eternal God in his uncreated Being. All symbols and images, and language itself, are *paradeigmatic*.

What we are concerned with here in both Irenaean and Athanasian thought is *propriety of images and language* in our talking about God, that is, in our theology. Indeed, the phrase should not be *talking about* God, for theological terminology is only formed in the dialogue which God conducts with us in Christ. Theology is essentially *talking with* God, and in this relationship in Christ finding our godliness.

This is where our second consideration (noted on page 29) *the theological understanding of parable*) is seen to be entwined with the content of theology and assumes its importance. Parables are essentially paradeigmatic. They contain not literal truth, but pointers to truth. They direct the mind elsewhere – to that which is lying beyond the capacity of bare human statement and explanation, and thus beyond the story itself. The Hebrew word for 'parable' (*mashal*) means 'a stumbling-block, a scandal, an enigma'. In Deuteronomy[7] and Jeremiah,[8] Israel itself is called a 'parable', both references being to the existence of Israel among the nations whither they were scattered. This means that in the existence of the Israelite the world sees what it is to be humanity in relation to the living God, and what the result of human disobedience or human obedience to God, is. Israel was a mirror set in the midst of the peoples so that all could gaze and come to know the grace of God by which this people were held. Israel was a parable for all to ponder.

So too were the parables of our Lord. In pointing to the same thing, the estate of man before God, parables in fact point to Him as the teller of them. The so-called 'Prodigal Son', for example, is in origin Christ himself, who, as the Father's Word left his heavenly home and came into the far country where he identified himself with human need and the judged condition of mankind, and then ascended back to the Father with forgiveness and restoration for all. They are shot through with Christological significance. They convey by imaged, or refracted, form, what cannot sufficiently be uttered directly.

This is true of all theological terminology. Its essential character as refracted, imaged or paradeigmatic language has to be appreciated. The very nature of the object which theology examines, the self-revelation of God, demands this. For this is not an event which can be subsumed in our understanding and explained. We may ask of this, and all the acts of God (and God is as he acts and acts as he is, and therefore in enquiring of the acts we enquire of his Being) 'when?', 'why?' 'whence?', 'whither?' – but not 'how?' To so ask would be to presume that we had the capacity to explain the Being of God, before whom even the seraphim veil their faces and the cherubim spread the covering of their wings.

This does not mean that we have to adopt a way of thinking about God on the basis of what he is not. Gregory Nazianzen pointed out that if we cannot say anything positive as to what God is, then we cannot say with any accuracy what he is not.[9]

Although we cannot fully comprehend God, yet our knowledge of him is firm and sure when it is grounded only in his self-revelation in Christ, for there it is grounded ultimately in the eternal Being of the God who acts for and towards and within his creation and creatures. This has every implication for talking about the nature of time and what is meant by eternity, and the relation of time to eternity. An understanding of time and eternity, for their conceptual formulation, is to be referred to and determined by the content of God's revelation. For here, as theology might claim, is the time and space where Creator and creature have a trysting place, and where that which created time, and which lies beyond the boundaries and nature of time, is revealed within time, thereby not only disclosing its eternal dimension but illuminating the nature of time itself as its source.

Christ is therefore regarded as the bridge between the incomprehensible and the comprehensible, the invisible and the visible, the immeasurable and the measurable,[10] for he is both the eternal One by whom all things were and are made by virtue of the Divine nature he shares with the Father and the Spirit, and one of his own creatures by virtue of his identification with us, as man in the Incarnation – his human nature.

The 'community of union' which we have with Christ is the work of the Holy Spirit. In the theology of Irenaeus, the Spirit is firmly related to the Word and to the Father. It is his role to take us by decree of the Father into participation in Christ and all that he has done. The doctrine of the Trinity is immediate to the doctrine of the Incarnation.

This is why Irenaeus places Baptism very firmly at the beginning of his *Demonstration of the Apostolic Preaching*. This is the seal of our knowledge of God in Christ through the Spirit, and the empowering of our godliness by the Spirit through Christ to the Father. Knowledge and conduct, truth and being, light and life, are the conjoined themes of Irenaeus's thought. For him, Christ is at once both Revelation and Reconciliation. There cannot be one without the other. Here too, in the insistence that truth and life are linked, have we an entrance into the question of the nature of temporal existence, of the fact that humanity is humanity in and with and characterised by time. Time, in whatever we may come to say about it, cannot be regarded as that which is divorced from our existence, and our existence as something apart from time.

There is an emphasis here on the unity and interaction of both the appropriateness of theological terminology and the appropriateness of Christian life and conduct, or, wider, the temporal appropriateness of all human existence. Both terminology and existence take their nature and quality from correspondence to the nature and quality of the Truth of God in Christ. The soul (which for Irenaeus includes the mind, the soul being the rational identity of man) and the body are inseparable. Man is the soul of his body and the body of his soul, or, he is an embodied soul and an ensouled body. Body and soul are concerned in their union in participation in Christ.

Behind this unity of Truth and action, word and deed, principle and life, lies the Irenaean insistence that God is as he acts and acts as he is. There is no disparity or contradiction between Act and Being in God. As soon as God wills he speaks, and as soon as he speaks his Word is accomplished. Moreover, the work of God is in correspondence to the sort of God he is. Creation is a work of Grace and Love, because God exists as a God of Grace and Love.

THE DOCTRINE OF RECAPITULATION

All this is the ground of what is called the *Doctrine of Recapitulation*. This doctrine is the hallmark of the theology of Irenaeus. This is a lamentably neglected doctrine. It speaks of the nature of creation in its relation with God in the Creator Word Who, in God's Grace and Love, became incarnate.

It therefore gives a vantage point from which creation can be viewed, and it shows some remarkable parallels of thought forms, where it has been taken up by modern theologians such as Karl Barth and T. F. Torrance, to the methods of thinking employed in post Einsteinian physics and pure science. (For this concord between theology and science, see T. F. Torrance's *The Ground and Grammar of Theology, Divine and Contingent Order, Theological Science, Christian Theology and Scientific Culture*, etc).

Recapitulation means the summing up of all things and time in Christ. Great care has to be exercised here, for recapitulation is not achieved because of Christ's Divine nature alone, nor by his human nature alone, but by the mode by which the human nature is united with the Divine. Because this humanity of Christ has no independent existence of its own ('Adoptionism' is thereby ruled out) but is given existence within its union with the Divine, it becomes in its identity with us a human existence with a particular significance. It is the focal point of all creation, partaking as it does of the realities of this world of time and things, because it is the human flesh and nature of the Word by whom all things were made. By what the Word made flesh is and does, all time and things are re-created, and have this recreated quality already present in him – which re-created nature will be openly revealed at his second Advent.

Behind this lie various areas of theological concern and emphasis in the thought of Irenaeus. It should be emphasised here that what we are concerned with primarily is not the specific question of the response of Christian belief, and looking at that response in terms of the Christian life, but the general statement of the objective fact, as Irenaeus claims, of God's Acts and Being and what this means for all creation and the existence and estate of all humanity in the midst of all creation.

(1) THE ESTATE AND VOCATION OF MAN AT CREATION

Man is regarded as an especial creation. Here the groundwork is laid for the later description of man as 'the crown of God's

creation'. Irenaeus notes that man *is formed by His own hands*.[11]
The phrase 'the hands of God'[12] is found frequently throughout
the works of Irenaeus. The description denotes the Word and the
Spirit, and emphasises creation by the whole Trinity.

But here we are concerned with the peculiar place of man in
creation. He is to be God's vice-regent on earth, having dominion
over all things in a way responsible to God and with regard to
the nature of God's handiwork in creation. Man therefore stands
at the boundary between Creator and creature, eternity and time,
heaven and earth. He is formed to *be like unto God*.[13] Man
therefore is the reason for all creation, and all creation is characterised by the person of man. It is a creation with man at its heart
and as its crown.

The same thought is found, for example in the *Apostolic
Constitutions*[14]

> And Thou hast not only created the world itself, but hast also
> made man for a citizen of the world, exhibiting him as the
> ornament of the world.

This too has a parallel in some recent scientific thought, where
the various levels of all creation are regarded as having a relativity
to man – c.f. the first chapter in T. F. Torrance's *The Ground
and Grammar of Theology*, though the authors of *The Arrow of
Time* (P. Coveney and R. Highfield) gently place a question mark
against such assertions (c.f. particularly, *The Arrow of Time*
pp. 102–103). Indeed, the criticism of these authors that this
'anthropic' principle, especially in its 'strong' form, is based on a
teleological view of creation, that is, that it has a purpose, can be
levelled against all that has been said about theological claims
above.

What we need to perceive is that these claims are inevitable in
theology, but that the value of such theological approach lies, for
our purposes, in raising questions which no other science can
ask. It is also seeing what the very basis of theology (which may
well be called an assumption by non-theological minds) that God
and man, Creator and creature, in their union in the Incarnation,
has to say about the nature of time, the source of time, and what
lies beyond this temporal dimension. It may well be deemed by
others to be an assumption, but there is no science whatsoever
that does not rest on an assumption, which is beyond the
capabilities of absolute proof.

We may assume that there is a purpose to all creation. It is equally an assumption that there is not. In the former, the Incarnation is the 'assumed' vantage point; in the latter other assumptions of different bases are made. Be this as it may, the Incarnation holds a prime place in Irenaeus's mode of approaching recapitulation, and of necessity this implies teleology.

Man, according to Irenaeus, enjoys a particular relation to God. In the sanctum which the Creator prepared for man, Paradise,

> the Word of God continually resorted thither, and walked and talked with the man, figuring beforehand the things that should be in the future, (namely) that He should dwell with him, and should be with men, teaching them righteousness.[15]

In this way, Irenaeus links the Incarnation to the creative act of God.

(2) RECAPITULATION AND ADAM

One of Irenaeus's apparent eccentricities (another is his claim that our Lord was about fifty when He was crucified) is that Adam was created as a child:

> it was necessary that he should grow, and so come to his perfection.[16]

What is implicit here is that man can only come to a perfection in a *community of union* with God through the Word. There is therefore, for Irenaeus the idea of that future perfection in that relation to the Word. That perfection is seen in the Incarnation, where He Who alone is the image of God (for He is what He images) is made man.

Adam is regarded as the recapitulation of the whole human race. He is

> the ancient formation, the archetype, the protoplasm.[17]

That is why when he falls, all fall with him. In a very real sense for Irenaeus, the story of Adam is the story of all mankind and every individual. This is why Irenaeus is so insistent that Adam himself is saved by Christ. In all this he has *Romans*, *chapter 5*, clearly in mind, where man in Adam and man in Christ, and therefore Adam in Christ, is set out in relationship. Christ sums up humanity, and therefore Adam, who is to be regarded as being saved by that summing up in Christ.

To emphasise this, Irenaeus draws all sorts of parallels between the story of the Fall and the event of the Incarnation – between man's creation out of the virgin soil of the earth, and the birth of the Blessed Virgin; between Eve and Mary[18] (though there is not any idea of a parallel salvation here; it is a but a sign of salvation). Between creation and the Incarnation there is the Fall of man, and the choice and history of Israel, in which God deals with the results of that fall. The history of Israel, including the giving of the Law to Moses, is the preparation for that coming fulfilment of perfection in Christ.

(3) RECAPITULATION AND ISRAEL

Christ himself fulfils the whole epic of Israel. He is born out of the womb of Israel, and gathers up in himself all the things of Israel which pointed to him as the coming One and the nature of his coming and saving work – the Law, the Temple sacrifices, Kingship, etc.

There is a recapitulation of the Old Covenant made by God with Israel in the New Covenant. For Irenaeus, all Israel and its purpose as a paradeigmatic entity is fulfilled, perfected and brought to a head in Christ. This is emphasised, at great length sometimes, in *Adversus Haereses*, and is also given much space in *Demonstration of the Apostolic Preaching*[19]

If it is dealt with but briefly here that is not to diminish its importance. It is one level of Recapitulation in the thought of Irenaeus – albeit a most important one, for it is the grounding of recapitulation in the realities of space and time – in the midst of his great view of the panorama of full recapitulation.

Irenaeus, however, delights in drawing out involved and de-tailed comparisons, in keeping with the exegesis of his time and its emphases. L. S. Thornton in his three volumes *Revelation and the Modern World*, *The Dominion of Christ* and *Christ and the Church*, spends too much time on this parellelism in Irenaeus between the Old and the New Covenants, with the result that the wider and more significant aspects of Irenaeus's doctrine are dealt with summarily and not grasped in their full implication.

(4) THE RECAPITULATION OF ALL THINGS IN CHRIST

The shortest setting out of the breadth of the doctrine of Recapitulation in Irenaeus is found in some of the surviving fragments of lost works, particularly *Fragments* LII and LIII. In these, the work of Christ is seen in ever expanding circles, from various elements within Israel, to all Israel, to the human race, to all the world and to all creation including the heavenly host.

Here we are at the Christological heart of the doctrine. The basis of this is that the flesh assumed by the eternal Word (that Word *semper co-existens filius patris* – the Son always existing with the Father) at the Incarnation is our Adamic flesh. This is emphasised throughout Irenaeus's sections on the subject in *Adversus Haereses*. That is to say, the reality of the eternity of God is brought to bear on the realities of time and things, where they stand in their alienation to God. These temporal and spatial realities, centring on our human flesh and nature are taken into inseparable union with the reality of the divine and eternal Word, and therefore in union with the Being which God is in all eternity. By this, the work of re-creation from within the realities of this creation is begun and completed. This is succinctly stated by Hippolytus also:[20]

> . . . That He might establish the holy orders of intelligent exist-ences in the heavens, in immutability by the mystery of His Incarnation, the doing of which is the recapitulation of all things in Himself. He remained, therefore, also, after His incarnation, according to nature, God infinite, and more, having the activity proper and suitable to Himself – an activity growing out of His divinity essentially, and manifested through His perfect holy flesh by wondrous acts economically [that is, by the establishing of order], to the intent that He might be believed in as God, while working out of Himself by the flesh, which by nature is weak, the salvation of the universe.

The effect of the eternal Word, by whom all things were made (and therefore to whom all things are already related by virtue of their creation by him) taking these realities and making them his own in assuming our flesh and nature, means that all time and all things are fundamentally affected by this. Their contingent rela-tion to him now becomes a matter of inseparable but unconfused (to use later, but here implicit, terminology) union with him. They do now indeed live and move and have their being as the things they were intended to be, in him.

One of the most important emphases in Irenaeus's thought is that creation is an act of the sheer grace of God. There is no compulsion for God to create – He is all sufficiency in himself. There is no compulsion from within God, he does not need anything. There is no compulsion from without, only God exists in all eternity. He creates in order to let another entity share his eternal glory. It is the self-same Word who created all things who re-creates all things. This demonstrates the constancy of God's love and grace towards his creation – his faithfulness.

The effect of this doctrine of Recapitulation, is that the claim is made that the new creation is already a reality in Christ, and man and from man all things, find their true identity in this relationship with him. This is by way of participation in the Word made flesh and all that he has accomplished for creation. Hence the Pauline thought that 'if anyone is in Christ he is a new creature' and 'we are dead with him and risen with him' and 'our life is hid in Christ with God', runs through Irenaeus's exposition of this doctrine.

All time and all things have been fundamentally dealt with – things past, present and to come. The phrase 'the fulness of time' as applied to the Incarnation means exactly that. All things are gathered up in Christ, and already have their new creation in him. In Christ *the end is joined to the beginning*.[21]

This joining of the end to the beginning is an intriguing concept. It is found also (among others) in Tertullian:[22]

> So too, the two letters of Greece, the first and the last, the Lord assumes to Himself, as figures of the beginning and the end which concur in Himself; so that, just as Alpha rolls on till it reaches Omega, and again Omega rolls back till it reaches Alpha, in the same way He might show that in Himself is both the downward course of the beginning on to the end, and the backward course of the end up to the beginning; so that every economy [that is, ordering], ending in Him through whom it began – through the Word of God, that is, Who was made flesh – may have an end corresponding to its beginning. And so truly in Christ are all things recalled to the beginning.

and Jerome[23] (writing of the incarnation):

> But once Christ has come at the end of time, and Omega passed into Alpha and turned the end into the beginning . . .

It is tempting at least to note the parallel between this and the theory of the 'singularity' (in astronomical terms) of the Big Bang at the beginning and the singularity of the 'Big Crunch' at the end!

What is emphasised here, as a result of Recapitulation, is that not only knowledge, but quality of life (Godliness) has been set out in Christ. Truth and Godliness are only achieved by a community of union with him. This does not mean that their objective reality lies only in Christian response. On the contrary, a community of union between Creator and creature, God and man, has been achieved in Christ as fact and event. Acknowledgement and appreciation of this may be the Christian response, but that is but an 'amen' to what is fact and event. It is not the ground of their objective reality, nor is its absence the nullification of the efficacy of what has been achieved in that fact and event. This fact and this event concern and affect all creation, Christian response or no Christian response. As with the fact and event of creation itself, whether we acknowledge it or not, it is there. Our denial or if will not make it disappear!

Recapitulation, for Irenaeus, is a cosmic event of salvation, centring on man. In this, the incarnation, death, resurrection and ascension of Christ, are indicated as determinative for that fulness of understanding. This must concern radically the concept of time, for all time, as that which characterizes the nature of all creation, it may be suggested, is recapitulated in Christ.

3
Creation, Incarnation and Light

WE MUST now look at the implications of the relation between incarnation, creation, man and time, as suggested by the doctrine of recapitulation.

We make an entrance to this question in what may seem to be a curiously detached medium and an anachronistic one at that. This approach is made through the works of Robert Grosseteste (c1170–1253). The reason for this is that the same problematic themes which underlie the observations of Irenaeus in this area confront Grosseteste and these he makes explicit in tackling them. It is a tantalising fact that the same considerations centring on this question were still to the fore one thousands years later and even then were not resolved.

This is not to suggest that Grosseteste was familiar with the writings of Irenaeus. Sir Robert Southern notes[1] that the Fathers cited by Grosseteste include (in descending order of the number of references) Augustine, Gregory (of Nyssa), Jerome, John of Damascus, John Chrysosotom, Ambrose, Basil and Origen. Grosseteste also cites Gregory of Nazianzus, though Southern's list only refers to 'Gregory'. There is no mention of Irenaeus. Grosseteste himself, in a passage concerning the question of whether the incarnation would have taken place had there not been the fall of man, expressly states:

> By these and other arguments it seems possible to conclude that God would have become Man even if man had never sinned. I confess I do not know if I am right, and I am afflicted by my ignorance on this matter. As I have said above, I do not remember if any authority has come to this conclusion, and I do not wish or dare to pronounce conclusively on so hard a question without express authority . . .[2]

As he is scrupulous in making reference to his sources, there is no need to suppose that Grosseteste used Irenaeus without acknowledgement, particularly when Irenaeus had, in his *Demonstration of the Apostolic Preaching* implicitly but clearly raised already this idea of the incarnation.[3]

Again, in the parallel observations of Irenaeus, that Man was created as a child without full understanding,[4] and Grosseteste, that Man did not have his potentiality fully developed at creation,[5] there is no hint that the latter was indebted to the former.

There were, of course, compendiums of Patristic proof texts to the hands of mediaeval writers,[6] but without absolute proof of the contents of such that Gosseteste may have had, and, if he did have, as to whether or not they noted the sources of such texts, it is impossible to affirm or deny any dependence on Irenaeus by Grosseteste. The problem of sources after Irenaeus, used by Grosseteste, and whether or not they had recourse to at least the theological trends of Irenaeus in this question of incarnation, creation, man and time, cannot be resolved either. The works of Bede, for example, studied by Grosseteste, make no reference to any Irenaean source, immediate or secondhand.

It would appear on balance, therefore, that the influence of Irenaeus had no direct bearing in the west by the time of Grosseteste as far as a familiarity with his actual works is concerned. The similar themes dealt with may reflect perennial problems arising for like-enquiring theological minds. However, the parallelism of the themes leaves much unanswered as to how far Irenaeus's influence had been effective, but unmarked as his particular achievement, through general theological debate by the 13th century, being diffused into earlier sources.

Notwithstanding this, the attempt to expose and tease out an answer to these questions by the later theologian stretches out the issues and brings to the surface much that underlies the mind of Irenaeus in his observations on incarnation, creation, man and time.

This is in the general context of the relation of Creator and creation, which, in the mind of Grosseteste is found exemplified in many and various ways, but all pointing to one inseparable bond in which the integrity of each is not only maintained but enhanced for the human mind.

In his *Hexaemeron*, perhaps the earliest of those works written between 1230 and 1235, Grosseteste, following Basil's *Hexaemeron*, seizes on the phrase 'in the beginning' at the head of his observations on creation. Here Grosseteste decisively parts company with Aristotle whose influence generally pervaded the thought of mediaeval scholars via the translations of the Arabic commentaries of Averroes and Avincenna, and concentrates on the biblical emphasis of *creatio ex nihilo*. He does this by insisting on the importance of the biblical phrase 'in the beginning'.

His argument against Aristotle and those philosophers who side with him in claiming that the world has no beginning in time, is stated clearly.[7] Such assertions, says Grosseteste

> *Quos unius vergi ictu percutit et elidit Moyses dicens: In principio*

> Moses, strikes and dashes to pieces with the blow of these words: In the beginning.

The phrase 'in the beginning' denotes for Grosseteste the relationship between Creator and creation. All things have a beginning by and from God. That is to say, there is a contingent relationship in which the whole of creation depends upon God for its beginning and existence – contingency *from* God. There is a total qualitative distinction between that which is created and he who creates, and yet there is a relationship. This is a complex matter in the writings of Grosseteste, and precision and care have to be exercised in any analysis of it.

We take one passage as an example from the *Hexaemeron*, for this illustrates the involved analogous way of thinking which permeates his observations on the relation between uncreated God and created realities.

> *Hec itaque tria Trinitatis exampla est invenire universaliter in omnibus. Inter res autem corporeas manifestissimum Trinitatis exemplum est ignis, sive lux, que necessario de se gignit splendorem; et hec duo in se reflectunt mutuum fervorem. In coniunctione autem corporei cum incorporeo, prima exampla sunt in formis sensibilibus, et speciebus formarum sensibilium generatis in sensibus, et intentione animi coniungente speciem genita in sensu cum forma gignente que est extra sensum. Et huius rei evidentior est examplacio in visu. Color enim rei colorate gignit de se speciem sibi similem in oculo videntis; et intencio animi videntis coniungit speciem coloris genitam in oculo cum colore gignente exterius; et sic unit gignens et genitum quod apprehensio visus non distinguit inter speciem genitam et colorem gignentem; fitque una visio ex gignente et genito et intencione copulante genitum cum gignente. Et similiter est ista trinitas in quolibet exteriorem sensuum.*[8]

Thus therefore there are three examples of the Trinity to be found universally in everything. Amongst bodily things the most manifest example of the Trinity is fire, or light, which by necessity begets splendour from itself, and these two reflect their mutual warmth. However, in the conjunction of the bodily with the incorporeal, the prime examples are in forms apprehended by the senses and in species of sensible forms generated in the senses, and by the intent of the mind the species begotten in the sense is yoked with the begetting form which is outside the sense. However the most evident example of these things is in the sight. For the colour of a thing begets as coloured the species similar to itself in the eye of the beholder; and the intention of the viewing mind conjoins the species begotten of colour in the eye with the external begetting colour; and thus begetter unites with begotten, because the apprehension of the sight does not distinguish between the begotten species and the begetting colour; and there is made one vision out of the begotten by the deliberate embrace of the begetter with the begotten. And this Trinity is similar in any exterior sense.

This rather involved argument sets out an analogy between the threefold nature of perception concerning the operation of light and the mind, the constituent parts of which are the object observed, the image of that object in the mind, and the process of the mind informed by light whereby the external object and the internal image are joined as one. Hence there is an analogy to the Father (the begetter), the Son (the begotten), and the binding embrace of the Holy Spirit uniting these two. But this is all a process of light, which in itself is analogous to that Uncreated light which God is.

This analogous treatment is found in everything which Grosseteste surveys. In his *Dicta* he elaborates on the analogy between the smallest and most insignificant object in the universe, the 'atom', that is, (perhaps better to avoid anachronistic present scientific meanings of the term) 'a particle of dust', as a mirror of the Creator, God in his Unity and Trinity. The 'atom' is a microcosm, a universe in miniature. It reflect the whole in its infinitesimal proportions, its containing of all geometric forms and mathematical constituents, its durance and its beauty of form. But as all this it images the Unity of God, for it is a simple object, and the Trinity of God in its potentiality, analogous to the might of the Father, its form of essence, analogous to the wisdom of the Son, and the union of potential and form, analogous to the Holy Spirit, binding the Father and Son together in love.

We have here another example of an implicit insistence of light – which insistence is found throughout Grosseteste's thought on this matter of the relation between God and creation. Light is involved for the 'atom' mirrors God in the human mind by the image which is conveyed to that mind. He concludes this section by stating that wherever we look, there is a mirror of God, not as necessary first cause only, but as a Trinity of power and wisdom in the bond of love.

This is not bare natural theology. All Grosseteste's endeavours, whether they are deemed by later commentators to be under the rather artificial headings of 'science, 'philosophy' or 'theology', are undertaken in the context of the Christian belief in which he was nourished and which he saw as the unitary meaning of all creation. McEvoy,[9] for example, does not stress constantly enough the fact that he was above all a theologian and a bishop of the Church, and, as a result, tends to give a surely unintentional impression that there is but a loose conjunction between what Grosseteste writes about various facets of creation, the means he employed to so engage himself, and his theology. On the contrary, for Grosseteste there was but one field of knowledge, all aspects of creation, redemption, Creator and Redeemer profoundly bracketed together.

That theology is stated within the matter of God's self-revelation in Christ as the Triune God. Nowhere does Grosseteste suggest that his 'scientific' observations are 'proofs' of God, apart from and in addition to that revelation. Rather, it is because God has revealed himself as the Triune God that we are able to appreciate the significance of these potencies, forms and relations within creation. They are pointers to what the substance of that revelation is and handmaids to it – proofs, not of God, but of the universal validity of the revelation of himself as this God and no other.

But Grosseteste's treatment of the relation of Creator to creation is not only by way of this procedure of analogy. There is an ontological relation between uncreated Light and light as created. It is on the basis of this that an analogy of operation is possible to maintain.

Southern notes[10] that

> his theology is an examination of the paths by which the operation of God can be traced downwards to the most minute objects in the universe and upwards to the divine nature itself. Each of these paths has two different modes: the first is symbolic; the second, for want of a better word, scientific.

The upward and downward movements are both under the

compulsion of the Word made flesh, God conjoining the realities of creation to himself in taking human flesh and nature. This is pointed to in his view of the creation and place of man as a rational being and therefore a creature of light, and above all in this constant, determinative theme of light. Light, man's place in creation, the downward movement from God and the upward movement to God, all come together in his treatment of the Incarnation – and raise the underlying question, implicit in Irenaeus, of the Incarnation and Time.

His concentration on the creation narrative of Genesis, on the Psalms and the Johannine writings, all with their emphases on light, is shown by the constant references to them in so many of his works. Light is that to which he constantly appeals, for in an interpretation of it is found that sublime conjunction between Creator and creature. It is the foundation of all things, binding them in mutual harmony and all with God.

> *Quapropter Deus, qui lux est, ab ipsa luce cuius tanta est dignitas merito inchoavit sex dierum opera.*[11]

> Wherefore, God Who is light, by that selfsame light which assuredly is the dignity of all things, laid the foundation of the six days' work.

In this section of the *Hexaemeron*, he eulogizes light and its properties, its beauty, its swiftness as the most transparent, most luminous form of matter, its directness, its creation as the first corporeal form, quoting and appealing to, almost exuberant to be in such company, Basil, Ambrose and Augustine of Hippo. All this is expanded in his treatise *De Luce*, which, it is clear from his more precise and elaborated descriptions of light, is a work later than his *Hexaemeron*.

Light, for Grosseteste, has a unique place in the universe, not only for its peculiar properties which are of supreme interest to natural science, even such as it was then in his expounding of it, but in the nature of these properties which he sees as a parable of the nature of God. Its constant action, its integrity with itself, its ability to reproduce itself instantly, its fundamental role through which all created things are dependent upon it, its direct pathway in moving in straight lines and in accordance to precise geometric rules – all these he saw as pointers to the God who is Light himself.

In the first part of *De Luce*, Grosseteste claims that the first form of corporeity, that is the facility to embody, is light itself. In the instant of creation, form and matter which are inseparable, are simple, that is they do not possess dimension. From this comes expansion in three dimensions. Since form and matter are inseparable, the argument runs, simple form may impart dimension and measurement to simple matter only by self-propagation and immediate spreading so that the two would expand simultaneously, as they must clearly do, there being no such thing as form without matter or matter without form. Light is the only thing which behaves in this way of self-generation. Corporeity, only if it is light itself, the first form, the purest and most transparent and subtle matter, can do this, otherwise this would pre-suppose its three-dimensional expansion according to another and subsequent form on which it would be dependent.

Grosseteste's argument would seem to be that light is the first creation; it is the basic, purest and simple form of matter; hence because it is light and the fundamental of all creation, creation is expanded and formed in this way.

At creation, light generates itself and expands from a single point without dimension. This we may call the Primordial Point. Light so multiplies itself from this point infinitely and equally in every direction that a sphere is formed, the boundaries of which are determined by the fact that at given limits the rarefaction of matter so dispersed can go no farther. This quality and action of light is given credence when its excellence, nobility and dignity, far exceeding the nature and properties of all other things, is considered and appreciated For all other things are the result of light, and are diverse, being more dense or less dense, heavier or lighter, of this property or that property, depending on their formation and dispersal by the actions and movement of light which are mathematically precise and patterned.

But the question arises as to this infinite multiplication of light and why it produced a cosmos of finite things. To answer this Grosseteste then embarks on an extremely involved mathematical exercise. That which is without dimension cannot produce quantity if multiplied a finite number of times (that is – and only as an entrance into this idea – 0 × 20 or 33 or whatever, is still 0). Therefore, an infinite multiplication is necessary (that is, a multiplication of an order qualitatively different from that of finite multiplication). One simple thing cannot be infinitely or indeed finitely greater than another simple thing, both having no dimension. But that which is finite exceeds a simple thing infinitely. Therefore, an infinite multiplication of a simple thing will lead to a finite extension of the simple thing into quantity. Thus light, a simple thing at the instant of creation, infinitely multiplied expands and extends matter, which in its first form as light is therefore originally a simple thing, into finite dimensions. This infinite multiplication is necessary to bridge the infinite gap between that which is simple and that which is finite. It does not result in the formation of an infinite thing, for the difference between simple and finite is itself infinite. This, then is the nature of the whole cosmos, in essence a simple point, yet, by light and by light's infinite operation, the sum of all subsequent realities.

It must be underlined that when speaking of the infinity of light's operation, Grosseteste is not equating light with the eternity which God is. He never speaks of the infinity of God. He is not confusing Uncreated Light with created light. Indeed it may be argued that 'infinity' for Grosseteste is more a comment on the limitation of the human mind than a category distinct from finitude. Infinity is finitude to an unknown and incalculable degree. It should be strongly suggested that Grosseteste's employment of such phrases as 'infinity' is a comment on the limitations of the mind and that he is not postulating categories totally distinct from the nature of the created order. Infinity is not that which lies beyond and is other than finitude, it is merely finitude immeasurable because of the limitations of the mind. Indeed he establishes the theory of relative infinities, which are ultimately relative to God.

That God is over and above and beyond even infinity and an infinity of infinities is set out clearly in Grosseteste's observation.[12]

> *Sicut enim que vere in se finita sunt, nobis sunt infinita, sic que vere in se sunt infinita, illi sunt finita. Iste autem omnia creavit in numero, pondere et mensura, et iste est mensurator primus et certissimus. Iste numeris infinitis, sibi finitis, mensuravit lineas quas creavit. Numero aliquo infinito sibi certo et finito mensuravit et numeravit lineam cubilem, et numero infinito duplo lineam bicubilem et numero infinito subduplo lineam semicubilem.*

> For just as those things which in fact are finite in themselves, and to us they are infinite, so things which in fact are infinite in themselves are finite to Him. Moreover, He created all things in number, weight and measure, so He is the prime and most certain

Mathematician. He, by infinite numbers, finite to Himself, measured the lines which he created. By means of some infinite
number, to Him fixed and finite, He measured and numbered a
line of one cubit, by a double infinite number a line of two cubits
and by a half infinite number a line of half a cubit.

This text follows *MS Marciana*. The use of 'cubilis' (a bed) is
curious. We may deduce that it is a scribal error for 'cubitas' (a
cubit) as this corresponds with the passage in *De Luce* VII, lines
27–35 in Ludwig Baur's edition of 1912, which deals with the
infinite multiplication of light, extending matter *in dimensionem
bicubitam* and going on to say that by the same double infinite
multiplication matter will be extended three cubits, and by half
extended in the dimension of one cubit.

CONTINGENCY: LIGHT, TIME AND HUMANITY

Behind the thinking on finite and infinite numbers, relative
infinities, and the claim that all infinity is but finite to God, there
lies the influence of Augustine of Hippo on Grosseteste. The
same train of thought is found in the former's *De Civitate Dei.*[13]
Certainly, like Augustine here, Grossteste appeals to the same
verse from Wisdom (XI:20) – 'Thous hast ordered all things in
number, measure and weight'. Augustine continues:

And the Saviour says in the Gospel, 'the very hairs of your head
are all numbered'.[14] Far be it from us then to doubt that all
number is known to Him 'whose understanding' according to the
Psalmist 'is infinite'.[15] The infinity of number, though there be
no numbering of infinite numbers, is yet not incomprehensible by
Him whose understanding is infinite. And thus, if everything
which is comprehended is defined or made finite by the comprehension of him who knows it, then all infinity is in some ineffable
way made finite to God, for it is comprehended by His
knowledge.

Lying further behind this may be the Plotinian thought of
Porphyry (c. 232–c. 303) in his mathematical treatises as part of
the Neo-Platonic residue in Augustine's thought. And beyond
Porphyry there may be the mathematician Nichomachus of
Geresa, who would seem to be the first to deal with the question
of finitude and infinity in this way.

Whatever the antecedents of Grosseteste's thought, the way in which he deals with the question of infinity and finitude in relation to light and the creative act of God is original and far-reaching.

There are two main implications to be stressed in this achievement apart from the consideration of the quality, nature and activity of light.

First, the underlying implicit principle of contingency. Creation is creation *ex nihilo*, and therefore everything is totally dependent upon God for its existence and order. But this contingency *to* God is held with contingency *from* God, for he affirms by his very act of creating (and particularly creating the universe as an entity of light) its own rationality, characteristic, dimension and nature. It has freedom to be itself in its own created identity, yet it has this freedom precisely because it is dependent on him. Contingency *from* can only be maintained in terms of contingency *to*. In other words, creation can only be created as such, and appreciation of it can only be true appreciation, when it is seen to be God's creation, and in relation to him in this twofold way.

The second implication is that a distinction has to be made perceiving and acknowledging the qualitative difference of the human mind, to which some things appear as infinite, and God himself, to whom what is even the infinity of infinities according to the measurement and limitation of the human mind, is finite. In other words, the subjective limitation of the mind has constantly to be held to the fore in all observations about the creative acts of God. There must be a necessary awe and reverence in dealing with the created realities as they unfold themselves in the majesty of their objective integrity, the mind being but the servant of that unfolding and disclosure. They are further linked inextricably, for light is the medium of the perception of that unfolding, both to the physical sight and to the mind in its enlightenment by the objective realities confronting it.

These two considerations state, generally, a doctrine of the created intelligibility of the universe which is not self-explanatory but is grounded beyond itself in the uncreated Intelligibility and Rationality of God. There is in Grosseteste's thought an absolute distinction between the Creator and the creature, between God in his eternal Being and created being. That is why he is so insistent that what may appear infinite to us is not to be confused with the immeasurability of God. All created infinities are but finite to him, for there is an absolute distinction in the way in which God calculates and the way in which we measure. His ways are not our ways, nor his thoughts ours.

It follows that there is also an absolute distinction between that Rationality which God is in himself and the created rationality of the universe, between uncreated light and that which is created light in both its physical and mental aspects. There is also, again, an absolute distinction between that order which God is in himself, existing in his interior and eternal relations as Father and Son, bound in the bond of eternal Love, the Holy Spirit, and that order which God bestows upon creation in its temporal and spatial existence.

Yet there is a relation between Creator and creature. It is God's creation, created to be in relation with him and to share his glory, and corresponding to him in the created dimension of its light, rationality and order which He has bestowed upon it. It is upheld and sustained by him.

Only in the appreciation of contingency to and from God (that is that creation is utterly dependent on God for its beginning and evolving and sustaining – contingency to – yet it is created by him as an entity qualitatively different from his eternal Being and Nature, having its own nature and identity – contingency from), can such unfolding and disclosure as to the true nature of the rationality of creation take place.

Light is the characteristic of all matter and therefore of all creation. This brings to the fore the question of the contingency of creation to and from God, and its analogous nature in its created dimension to the divine nature. Creation is rational, in its spatial and temporal dimension, as God is Rationality itself. Light is the principle of rationality. God, as uncreated Light itself is uncreated Rationality. Creation is characterised by created light as the first creative act of God, and is therefore created rationality.

The first chapters of Book I of his *Hexaemeron* emphasise the Trinity, the relation of the Son to the Father, and the relation of creation and its intelligibility through the Son to the eternal Being of the Triune God. The incarnation stands central in Grosseteste's thought here, and particularly in terms of light.

The eternal Son is that Light, uncreated and eternal. The oneness of the Father, Son and Holy Spirit is stressed, appeal being made to Christ's own words as reported by St John:

. . . quod Filius Verbum sit unum in substancia cum Patre, et per consequens cum Spiritu Sancto. Quam unitatem substancialem expressit Filius cum dixit: Sicut et tu Pater in me et ego in te.

. . . Because the Son Word is one in substance with the Father, and in consequence with the Holy Spirit. Which unity of substance the Son expresses when He says: For Thou Father art in Me and I in Thee.[16]

The Incarnate Christ is the subject matter and endeavour of *that most sacred wisdom which is called theology.* Here we perceive that uncreated Light within the created dimension, and so have an entrance into the eternal Being of God.

That this stands foremost in Grosseteste's *Hexaemeron* is significant. Not only is he following the priority of Basil and Ambrose in their like works, but he is emphasising the direction of all theological thought concerning creation and putting it in its necessary context. Creation can only be understood in reference to the Incarnate Word, one with the Father and the Holy Spirit. The rationality and intelligibility of creation can only be perceived in the light of the Incarnation and the Trinity.

Here the place and role of light comes to the fore. The *fiat lux*, let there be light, is uttered by the Word who in the unity of the Father and the Spirit, is uncreated Light himself.

Grosseteste's emphasis on light, its primacy, its nature, its role, highlights contingency particularly as it results in the doctrine of the created intelligibility of the universe in its contingent relation to God. While the Son's relation to the Father is eternal Light from eternal Light, so too, creation's relation to Father and Son is created light by eternal Light. In Grosseteste's thought there is no Arian confusion between the eternal generation of the Son from the Father and the act of creation. Creation, typified by light, may be the work of the Son or Word of God, but it is the work of the eternal Son or Word in all His Godness and as Eternal Light. Nor has he made the Aristotelian assumption about the eternity of the world. It is created. It has a beginning. It is contingent to. It depends on the Creator Word and uncreated Light. It is not the Word or that Light in eternal dimension. It is contingent from. It has its own dimension as that which is created and therefore temporal and spatial, its own quality, nature and identity.

It is necessary to note here that in the employment of terminology expressing the relation between creation and Creator, Grosseteste is clear that while we employ verbal images out of the experience and circumstances and bounds of the created order (for we have no other language), these statements and symbols and images are but paradeigmatic. They do not convey the created content, with its limited meanings, into God. This he notes in his *Commentary on the Celestial Hierarchy*, where in chapter two he discusses the divine and angelic names. The sequence of his thesis is that because of the qualitative distinction between God and all things created, whether earthly or heavenly, all things are negated when it comes to speaking appropriately of God.

He is not advocating a *via negativa* approach to God, for if we cannot say what God is,[17] then equally we cannot say what God is not. When we positively apply attributes to God, we must beware that these are not applied literally, for this would be a confusion between the Creator and the creature. In the fifteenth chapter of the *Commentary*, he enunciates this more substantially by insisting that all verbal images and symbols must be cleansed from their created content and material implications and associations.

Behind the Arian heresy of the fourth century, with its confusion of the act of creation with the eternal generation of the Son from the Father, there lay this mistake, which Grosseteste shuns, of using verbal images and statements about God unreformed and unburdened of their temporal content. Equally, if there was adherence to the Aristotelian idea of the eternity of the world, which Grosseteste denies, language became endowed with eternal significance and did not require the scrutiny as to its propriety which he, and, for example, Irenaeus, Athanasius and Gregory of Nyssa so long before him, strongly advocated.

Verbal images, symbols and words themselves, have to be bent out of their day-by-day application to serve as pointers to a dimension qualitatively 'over' and 'above' and 'beyond' this created temporality and spatiality determining the limitations and boundaries of human existence and mental endeavour. They are helpful to man *rather than fitting to God*.[18]

We may now gather together these areas noted above. Light, according to Grosseteste, is created as a simple thing, what we have called a 'primordial point'. We may indeed apply the terminology of astrophysics and call it a *singularity*. In its created dimension, light is contingent to and from the Creator who is uncreated Light. It is not that Light, but is, in its created quality, nature and attributes, both the most appropriate analogy to uncreated Light as a pointer to it, and the closest approximation to the Nature and Attributes of its Creator.

If we take Grosseteste's observations about the extension of light from its creation as a Primordial Point, a singularity, through its extension by what is infinite calculation to the human mind but, to the Creator merely a finite action, so that it is the ground and content of all things that are created, then we are left with the thought that at that 'primordial point' that instant *fiat lux*, all things created are present. Here we have a relation between time and light in the sense of instantaneous creation. If it is the purest form of matter, and creation is the extension of that Primordial Point, then all matter is contained in that Point – and all time.

Of the Fathers with whom Grosseteste was certainly conversant, Gregory of Nyssa states this succinctly: [19]

> All, I say, with any insight, however moderate, into the nature of things, know that the world's Creator laid time and space as a background to receive what was to be; on this foundation He builds the universe. It is not possible that anything which has come or is now coming into being by way of creation can be independent of space and time. But the existence which is all-sufficient, everlasting, world-enveloping, is not in space, nor in time; it is before these, and above these in an ineffable way; self-contained, knowable by faith alone; immeasurable by ages; without the accompaniment of time; seated and resting in itself, with no associations of past or future, there being nothing beside or beyond itself, whose passing can make something past and something future. Such accidents are confined to the creation, whose life is divided with time's divisions into memory and hope. But within that transcendent and blessed Power all things are equally present as in an instant: past and future are within its all-encircling grasp and its comprehensive view.

That all things and all time are created instantly, being present to God, does not destroy the concept of contingency. For it is here that the Incarnation should be related to creation inseparably. Let us tease this relation out.

Primarily, we must be aware here of the limitations of language. Grosseteste we have noted claimed that the question of whether or not the incarnation would have happened had there not been a fall of man, was beyond his mind. His problem is essentially one

of language and time-concepts, and it seems to be on this basis
that he departs from the question leaving it unsatisfactorily and
tantalisingly suspended, not having come to a workable system of
applying temporal terms to indicate time/eternity relativity. He
does say that the whole question revolves round the fact that it
entails the subjection of all things to the *Man-God.*[20] Again, in
dealing with the creation of man as the image of God, requires

> an account of the relationships between God and Man and all
> other things. Such an explanation is not to be expected from any
> human being; how much less from one so inexpert as I am. A
> man could no more explain these things than a point could
> explain a line, or a grain of sand the sands of the sea-shore, or a
> drop of rain the water of the ocean, or an atom the system of the
> whole world. Nevertheless what God will deign to give me, I
> will stammeringly set forth briefly in such words as I have.

Grosseteste is quite well aware of the limitations of the mind
and how it expresses itself, and of the challenge before it to speak
appropriately from within these limitations of that which confronts the mind from without temporal and spatial boundaries.

We may take the example of the often used word 'before'.
'Before' is a temporal term, but such terms have to be employed
in speaking of the creative acts of God. We have no language of
eternity, so therefore we are reduced absolutely to the constriction
of such phrases as 'Before time began'. We have to mark well the
limitations of language here, and employ such terms by consciously bending them out of their normal usage. 'Before' and
such like terms require to be emptied of their temporal content,
otherwise we project time into eternity and end with the (already
popular) concept that eternity is endless time, a time before time
ad infinitum.

The dilemma of using 'before' unreservedly is illustrated by
the Fathers of the Church dealing in particular with the Arian
heresy of the fourth century. We may take as but one example
Ambrose, who in combating the idea that there was a time when
the Son of God was not, that is, a time when he did not exist as
the eternal Son of the Father in the unity of the Holy Spirit,
sees this confusion as a result of the projection of temporal and
spatial concepts into God, and writes:[21]

> Tell me . . . whether there was ever a time when God Almighty
> was not the Father and yet was God. 'I say nothing about time',
> is your reply. Well and subtly objected! For if you bring time into

the dispute, you will condemn yourself, seeing you must acknowledge that there was a time when the Son was not, whereas the Son is the ruler and creator of time. He cannot have begun to exist after His own work. You must needs allow Him to be the ruler and maker of His work.

'I do not say', you answer, 'that the Son existed not before time'; but when I call Him 'Son', I declare that His Father existed before Him, for as you say father exists before son'. But what does this mean? You deny that time was before the Son, and yet you will have it that something preceded the existence of the Son ... that the generation from the Father was a process in time. For if He began to be a Father, then, in the first instance He was God, and afterwards He became a Father. How then is God unchangeable? For if He was first God and then the Father, surely He has undergone change by reason of the later and added act of generation ... Cease then to apply to the Godhead what is proper only to created existences ...

Again, we may cite Gregory of Nyssa, who clearly sees the dilemma and acknowledges the unavoidable use of concepts such as 'beneath':

The Divine nature is a stranger to these special marks of creation: It leaves beneath itself the sections of time, the 'before' and the 'after', and the ideas of space: in fact 'higher' cannot properly be said of it at all.[22]

This limitation of language is felt severely in trying to say that instantaneous creation does not over-rule the principle of contingency. For we are faced here with trying to describe the content of creation from God's side, as it were. We cannot say all things exist in the mind of God and then are brought into being piece by piece and part by part. That is to project temporal concepts into the deity, presuming a time lapse between God thinking and God acting. The thought of God is the accomplished deed. As soon as (another temporal phrase) God thinks, he acts. This is brought out by Basil in his *Hexaemeron* where he deals with the speech of God as His creative act.[23]

Let there be light. The order itself was an operation, and a state of things was brought into being ... It must be understood well that when we speak of the voice, of the word, of the command of God, this divine language does not mean to use a sound which escapes from the organs of speech, a collision of air struck by the tongue; it is a simple sign of the will of God, and, if we give it the form of an order, it is only the better to impress the souls whom we instruct . . . The word is not limited to a simple command. It lays down the reason necessitating the structure of the firmament . . . Let us ask how God speaks. Is it in our manner? Does His intelligence receive an impression from objects, and after having conceived them, make them known by particular signs appropriate to each of them? Has He consequently recourse to the organs of voice to convey His thoughts? Is He obliged to strike the air by the articulate movements of the voice to unveil the thought hidden in His heart? Would it not seem like an idle fable to say that God should need such a circuitous method to manifest His thoughts? And is it not more comfortable with true religion to say that the Divine will and the first impetus of the Divine intelligence are the Word of God?

Here we have the assertion that the instant will, thought, 'word' and act of God *are* the Word of God himself. The action of God is a Trinitarian statement. His acts and his being are one in the order which God is eternally, and as he externally expresses himself in his works.

The difficulty we have is to empty of their material content scrupulously all our concepts of time and space in applying them to the eternal Being of God. We cannot conceive even in an analogous way *how* God exists. God, as we are reminded by Athanasius, is *beyond comparison.*[24]

Equally we cannot even begin to articulate the way in which God works, save to say that the creation which he calls into being out of nothing, must correspond in its particular dimension to what God eternally is in himself. That is why it is above all an intelligible, ordered creation characterized by light.

Contingency is this relationship of creation to Creator. If we say that God is 'over' and 'beyond' and 'above' time, this does not mean that he is 'timeless' – a word to be shunned as so negative that it is meaningless. Nor does it mean that he is 'over' and 'above' and 'beyond' all being. He is Being who holds all being in relation to himself as its Creator. Equally he holds all time to himself, for to create means consequentially to bring time into being.

But if contingency to and from God is taken seriously, this will demand that we see that the opposite is not true: namely, that God is contingent on creation. It is the position of the orthodox faith that God has no need of anything. He is in himself, in his

Triune existence, all sufficiency, company, majesty, light and love. There is no internal compulsion upon God to create, as though he needed to fulfil himself.

Nor is there any external pressure on him to create. He alone exists eternally, indeed is 'eternity'. There is not an independent dimension called 'eternity' which God happens to occupy; rather because God's Being is eternal there is eternity as his dwelling 'place'. There is nothing else existing external to God to compel him to form it into creation. This would be to posit a theory of the eternity of matter, for example, and end up in a dualism, whereby God was not alone in eternity, but existed alongside something else.

Here we may consider again the tentative observations on the Incarnation by Irenaeus and Gosseteste as to whether or not that would have taken place if there had been no fall of man. And again we may come to the idea that the creative act of God centres on the Incarnation of the Word by whom all things are created.

If it is said that the Incarnation took place only because man fell, the spectre which arises is the implication that God must be contingent on the fact of sin and evil. Did God create that, namely humanity, which, as it were, went out of control and unleashed evil on account of which God realized that he had to act and do something? What does this say about the Divine omniscience? Was God ignorant of the potential of what he had created? Did he not foresee the possibility of evil, and if so, why did he wait so long to do anything about it?

It could be said that these questions project temporal concepts and spans into the existence of God. The real question which is not asked is: 'What is the relation of the time which God creates to his eternity?' Barth's division of time into God-created time, our time and the time of revelation at first sight would appear to be this projection. But it is not in substance. For his insistence that time can only be understood in terms of Revelation time, that is the time which God has for us, goes straight to the heart of the matter, but, I would suggest, not quite in the way in which Barth intended it to do so. His observation is correct, but his application does not go far enough.

This is where I would wish that Barth had not been so quick to reject his former emphasis in his *Commentary on the Epistle to the Romans* of crisis and tension, and had carried some of that mode of thought into this issue of time in relation to God, and particularly what this means for the bringing about of the existence of time as things are created. There is generally lacking the sense of crisis in creation, that is, what it involves for the Being of God.

Implicit in the quotation previously given from Irenaeus's *Demonstration of the Apostolic Preaching*, is that the Incarnation would have taken place even if man had not sinned. The Word of God, according to Irenaeus's time sequence of creation, walks and talks with man in Paradise before the fall, revealing to him the union of God and man, the perfection of humanity, which will be. The text does not contain any cognition of the fall about to take place. Such tutelage by the Word of God is part of the man's upbringing, he being created a child. There is only set before him the creative intent of God to share his glory with his creature, God taking humanity to himself and dwelling with them and they with him. This is the content of the conversing of God and man by the Word of God.

Grosseteste begins his particular contribution to this debate with the centrality of man in creation. Man, for him was a microcosm, and he uses the symbol of a smaller circle within a larger (a microcosm within a macrocosm) to indicate this idea in the authorities he claims for support. (His index consisted of a series of appropriate symbols in the margins of his manuscripts.) His manuscript of Gregory's *Moralia*[25] contains the symbol and it is found against his list of such authorities.[26] He views the realities and component parts of the universe not only in their natural significance, but as symbolic instructors of mankind. They teach man lessons about the relation of creation to God in their respective places and functions, form and substance, being and acts.

This universal imagery of all creation was on behalf of man, as indeed was the existence of all created things. This principle of *Quod omnia propter hominem* was based on a solitary text from Deuteronomy – chapter 4, verse 19 – according to his index in *Bodley MS 198*. But it was also based on the general interpretation of texts such as the creation narrative in Genesis, Psalm 8 and like passages. The centrality of man for Grosseteste was founded on the twofold fact that man is created in the image of God and is given dominion over all the orders of creation.

This, however, is not just a statement about the role, place, vocation and estate of man in the created orders. It is the fundamental principle lying behind the creative plan of God. It is a basic statement of the nature of the whole universe and all which composes it, centred as it is on the existence of humanity. It is construed as the decree of God as to the purpose of his creation. It is seen as the reason why God created. As such it is the eternally decided 'building-block', the headstone, for God's creative act.

His doctrine of the centrality of man is expounded in extended form in his *Hexaemeron*.[27] In this section he sees the unity of the diversity of all creation as residing in God, hence his findings of Trinitarian analogies in all things from a speck of dust to light itself. He insists that the universe must have a principle of unity whereby it so resides. In the same way as the microcosm, the body of man, has such a unifying factor, which is the heart, animating man and sustaining him in life, so the macrocosm must similarly have such a factor – otherwise it is a chaotic diversity without essential form or purpose. The question is: 'what is that factor of unity?'

Grosseteste was deeply influenced here by the argument in two of Aristotle's works, on both of which he wrote commentaries: the *Posterior Analytics* and the *Physics*. Of these, the first influenced him with regard to the processes by which general laws are deduced from the observation of particular events and circumstances. The second engraved in his mind the idea that all development and evolution of things were present potentially at the inception of the framework in which they happen. This spoke out to him with regard to creation, and in particular concerning the estate and place of man.

The full potentiality of man is his union with God, the sharing of humanity, without losing its identity and nature, in the Divine life. Here the Incarnation becomes paramount in Grosseteste's considerations. Not only is the union of God and man in Christ the means whereby, through communion with him, humanity finds its union with God, but Christ himself, being the express image of God and imaging what he is himself,[28] is that unifying factor.

Nature's unity cannot be provided by God as he exists eternally; for he is outwith creation. Nor can it find its unity in man by himself, because it requires a *singularity* in order to establish it and humanity is diverse in the multitude of its individuals.

Moreover, creation requires to find its unity in and through and by something greater than itself. Only God holds this dimension and stature, but, again, he is outside creation.

Yet mankind must in some way be involved as a unifying factor because of its vocation and estate as made in the image of God, being the vice-regent of God in its dominical power and authority over creation – and the fact that all things are created for man. Man is the last work of God and in a sense is the recapitulation of all else created, the sum of all that was worked on the previous days. Yet man is not greater than the whole.

But God and Man in union fulfils all the necessary requirements to bind creation together – God greater than creation and man participating in it. Hence the Incarnation which is, for Grosseteste, the highlight, the goal, and therefore the foundation of creation.

This is why he suggests, albeit tentatively, that the Incarnation would have occured even if man had not sinned. It was the *terminus a quo, terminus ad quem* of creation. Here there is a parallel with Irenaeus's insistence that Christ *joined the end to the beginning.*[29]

Southern[30] writes that in Grosseteste's view, the

> Incarnation, therefore, was the necessary conclusion to the work of creation.

Perhaps it is rather more in the mind of Grosseteste. Or, at least, was he moving towards the idea, which seems to be necessarily implicit in all this, that the Incarnation is the essential corollary of creation, which creation finds to be its fulfilment and destiny and purpose, or indeed, that creation is the corollary of Incarnation, the latter being the touchstone of the former?

What seems to be lying dormant here is the idea that Christ himself is the Beginning and the End, the Alpha and the Omega, the Archetype and the Completion, the Original Form and the Recapitulation of all that exists as creation.

This is not to say with the Arian heresy of the fourth century (and the Gnostics beforehand) that Christ's Divinity as the Word of God, is Itself a created thing or even the first and prime of all creatures. The Word of God is the One through whom all things are made, of one substance with the Father and the Spirit, God in all his Godness, and himself is the source of time on whom all time and things depend. There is not 'a time when he was not', as the Arians would have had it. He is, as Athanasius insisted the Ἀρχή ὁδῶν, the Beginning of ways, but not within the dimension of these 'ways'[31]

We may take stock of phrases employed by the Fathers to point to the Person or work of the Word Eternal and Incarnate, such as that which particularly Athanasius in his works against the Arians stressed, 'the Beginning of ways', and ask if there is a dimension of meaning which goes beyond that Patristic usage. Can they be the vehicles of pointing to something more than that particular Patristic deployment at that time?

This does not mean that we can take such phrases and bend them to any meaning convenient to any individual view or indeed collective view convenient to what is seen as cultural relativity. Nor does it mean that Patristic terminology is to be seen as a quarry for demythologising. It does mean that their meaning may be expanded in strict terms of their original usage as theological understanding unfolds more and more in accordance with the terms of the object of its study, in this case the doctrines of Creation and Incarnation. In this way they are used surely with the intent of the original authors and not placed in an historical straightjacket, albeit with their historical significance still emphasised, and are part of the substance of the living faith.

The term *Ἀρχή*, *Archē*, Beginning, is widely used by the Patristic authors. The various commentaries on, and many references to, the biblical account of creation refer it to the beginning of time and things. We have already seen Grosseteste's underlining of the importance of Basil's insistence on the fact that the creation has a beginning, as opposed to the idea of the eternity of the world. But it also has a significance when applied to God and to the Word of God in creative activity. Here it is supplemented by the word *ὁδῶν*, *hodōn*, of ways – the Beginning of ways.

The Patristic deployment of the phrase was generally against all Gnostic and Arian confusion of the act of creation with the generation of the Son or Word from the Father – that confusion which saw the Son or Word as having a beginning. The Fathers are scrupulous in their interpretation of the phrase which comes from Proverbs VII:22, and refers to the Wisdom of God in creation.

It is in this very scrupulosity that a legitimately wider and deeper application than that intended against particular historical heresies may become apparent. For such is the striving after precision that various possibilities may be seen to lie dormant and, at the time of their first application, unexpressed and unapplied for broader concerns.

Commenting on Proverbs VIII:22, Justin Martyr remarks[32] that

> You perceive . . . if you bestow attention, that the scripture has declared that this Offspring was begotten of the Father before all things created; and that which is begotten is numerically distinct from that which begets, any one will admit.

It is interesting here that Justin Martyr qualifies the use of *before* by the observation of arithmetic distinction, so that the 'before' of *before all things* is qualitatively different from the *before* when applied to temporal sequence within creation. In this he anticipates Augustine and Grosseteste in their numerical observations.

In a previous section[33] he specifically speaks of the Word of Wisdom as *Beginning*.

Irenaeus dwells largely on Proverbs VIII:22 and joins his comments in a passage[34] reminiscent of his *Demonstration of the Apostolic Peaching*, XII (which is probably the precis of this passage in *Adversus Haereses*) to his emphases that this Selfsame Word, begotten anterior to time and things, who with the Spirit is the Hands of God the Father in creating, became incarnate to

> join the end to the beginning, that is, man to God . . . in order that man . . . might pass into the glory of the Father.

Previously[35] Irenaeus dwells on the incapacity of man to measure God's hand in which the heavens are meted out, and resorts, as Justin Martyr did, to mathematic distinctions between the compass of God and the compass of human ability. In this section, relative infinities – the impossibility of measuring the heavens – *recount the endless multitude of cubits* – and the greater impossibility of measuring the Creator of the heavens, are implied. The loving decree of this immeasurable God to be the God of creation and particularly of man is set out by Irenaeus.[36]

> The glory of God is a living man; and the life of man consists in beholding God.

Man so beholds God in God's terms in the Incarnation, in which man may understand:[37]

the Invisible becoming visible, the Incomprehensible being made comprehensible.

But he still remains the Invisible and the Incomprehensible, for he still exists[38] *in the bosom of the Father* while yet incarnate.

The Incarnation for Irenaeus is the assumption of Adamic flesh and nature. He insists on this as the Word taking to himself all the limitations, follies, needs and judged nature of humanity of which Adam is the biblical recapitulation. The end of this is the bringing of creation with man at its heart and as its crown into a unity of communion with God. This is the creative intent of God, that man and creation may share His glory, this being their fulfilment. But the terminology used of this assumption of Adamic nature and flesh is significant. In the first place, Irenaeus insists[39] on the salvation of Adam in that assumption of Adamic flesh and nature. Adam for him is the recapitulation of all humanity, and, if Adam be not saved, then humanity is not.

What is assumed by the Word at the Incarnation is described variously as *the ancient formation, the protoplast, the archetype.*[40] These suggest a significance more than a description of the temporal priority of the recapitulative patriarch of the human race. Irenaeus is insistent on the significance of *Let us make* in the Genesis account of creation as opposed to the *Let there be* of all other orders of creation.

> But man He formed with His own hands [that is, the Word and the Spirit], taking from the earth that which was purest and finest, and mingling in measure His own power with the earth. For He traced His own form on the formation, that that which should be seen should be of divine form: for (as) the image of God was man formed and set on the earth.[41]

But which manlike form has God save the form of Jesus Christ? It seems to me that there is open here a wider and yet a more particular interpretation concerning the Image of God. There is a significant passage in *Adversus Haereses* in which Irenaeus counters any idea that other than God Himself was needed to achieve the work of creation. He condemns those who liken God to needy human beings, for God is all sufficient in himself having need of nothing.[42] He goes on to write:

> But He Himself in Himself, after a fashion which we can neither describe nor conceive, predestinating all things, formed them as

> He pleased, bestowing harmony on all things, and assigning them
> their own place, and the beginning of their creation . . . He
> formed all things by His Word that never wearies.

With this we ought to consider another passage:[43]

> Let them cease, therefore, to affirm that the world was made by
> another other; for as soon as God formed a conception in His
> mind, that was done which He had thus mentally conceived.

Irenaeus here removes any suggestion of temporal sequence in
the thought and act of God, that the latter follows the former at a
lapse of time. The thought of God and the action of God is
'instantaneous'. The use of this term does not imply that its
temporal content should be regarded, and therefore, a temporal
interpretation applied; it is the only suitable word we have. In
the same way he writes[44] of God's instant thinking and speaking
the thought, so that the Word is not divorced in any way from
the mind of God, but acts in 'instant' harmony. We are not to
transfer to God the limitations of our thinking and speaking with
the lapse of time and the weak effect between our thoughts and
words. Our thoughts and words have a beginning and a sequence.
God does not.[45]

But if Christ is THE Image of God, for he is what he images,
then do not the phrases *protoplasm*, *archetype*, *first formation*
refer in the first instance of Christ himself? That is to say, is
God's conception of creation centred on Christ, the Word made
flesh? In the omniscience and omnipotence of God this must
surely be so, otherwise we are forced to the conclusion that God
at creation did not know what he was unleashing with regard to
evil and sin, and is contingent on these, having to act at a later
time as a result of their presence in creation.

If, however, God knows what creation will 'cost' him, is it not
that we may argue that he 'instantly' joins the end to the
beginning, and there is, from the side of God in a constant
present, the fact and event of the Word made flesh, the beginning
and end of Incarnation?

4

Time and Light: the Beginning

WE HAVE come to the consideration that creation and Incarnation are profoundly bracketed together in the creative counsel, act and accomplishment of God in saying *Let there be*, *Let us make*. The alternative is to see eternity, that is the existence of God, as endless time. This leads into the confusion that there is a time before creation. But time requires space and motion; therefore God must exist as we exist, in the same qualitative dimension, but only greater with regard to quantity. Irenaeus brings out the essential difference between God's existence and mode of operation and our being and way of working, warning of the inadequacy of our terminology when we think on such things.[1]

> Just as he does not err who declares that God is all vision, and all hearing (for in what manner He sees, in that also He hears; and in what manner He hears, in that also He sees), so also he who affirms that He is all intelligence, and all word, and that, in what respect He is intelligence, in that also He is word, and that this Nous is His Logos, will still indeed have an inadequate conception of the Father of all, but will entertain far more becoming [thoughts regarding Him] than do those who transfer the generation of the word to which men give utterance to the Word of God, assigning a beginning and course of production [to Him], even as they do to their own word. And in what respect will the Word of God – yea, rather God Himself, since He is the Word – differ from the word of men, if He follows the same order and process of generation?

Again Irenaeus seems to counter the idea that God exists in endless time in his argument against those who ask 'What was God doing before he created?'

> If, for instance, anyone asks 'What was God doing before He made the world?' we reply that such an answer lies with God Himself. For that this world was framed perfect by God, receiving a beginning in time, the Scriptures teach us; but no Scripture reveals to us what God was employed about before this event. The answer therefore to that question remains with God, and it is not proper for us to aim at bringing forward foolish, rash and

blasphemous suppositions [in reply to it]; so, as by one's imagining that he has discovered the origin of matter, he should in reality set aside God Himself Who made all things.

In this section the phrase *was framed perfect* is of significance. the word translated by it – ἀποτελεστικός, *apotelestikos* – would seem to indicate that it was produced fulfilled or that all its potential was present. That this fulfilled or complete potential was set as a beginning, and therefore found a temporal form, would seem to be a reasonable interpretation.

What may be deduced here in bringing all the above observations to bear, is that we are faced with drawing out a concept of the *beginning* as the fulness of time and things, which beginning and fulness is refracted through time, but which nevertheless is a constant present to God.

We again may think here of a single beam of light and that beam refracted into its constituent colours. The singularity is on the side of God as he creates, the refractions are the diversity of creation and the succession of aeons, centuries, decades, years, days, hours, through which humanity lives and moves and has its being – that is, our perception. All time and all things are present to God in the instant of creation.

There is clearly a fine distinction here between this concept and the notion of the eternal generation of the universe which theology has discarded. The position here is not that of Origen who could not think of God as the Almighty Creator of all, except in necessary eternal conjunction with all things.

But however fine the distinction, there is nevertheless a qualitative difference. First it must be made clear that there is no confusion between the eternal begetting of the Word by the Father in the interior and eternal relations of the Godhead and the act of creating that which is temporal and external. The Father is always the Father, but not always Creator, as Athanasius points out.[3] His nature as Father of his Son or Word is constant; his will to be Creator is secondary. For God to create is secondary, for this is a matter of his will; for God to beget his Word and therefore be always Father is primary, for this is a matter of his nature.

> If He frames things that are external to Him and before were not, by willing them to be, and becomes their Maker, much more will He first be Father of an Offspring from His proper Essence.

The Word by whom all things were made by the Father in the

power of the Spirit, is firmly within the eternal Being as the Nature of God. That which is made, all created things, have a beginning. We may say (for we have no other words to express it) that all things were in the mind of God before he brought them into being and gave them a beginning – but the stricture here is that we cannot project temporal concepts into the Being of God and thereby mean literally by this that there was a lapse between God's mind thinking of creation and the act of creation itself.

Second, the application of temporal terms in speaking about the eternity of God and the relations and work of the Trinity, must be carefully scrutinized. As has been stressed, time-related conditions must not be read into God's Being, but this is the way, and the only way, in which our language and the thoughts so expressed are formed. We have to distinguish between their usage when applied to creation and when used of the Creator, for, in the latter, we are at the 'place' where even the cherubim veil their faces and the seraphim spread the covering of their wings. Such language is used in one sense in the one case, but bent out of its customary and common usage in the other.

The phrase *in the beginning* has to be understood of that which he has created which is given a beginning, and time subsequent to that beginning. But it is also understood of the creative act of God itself. Is there then a 'beginning' in God who by definition is 'without beginning'?

The *beginning* certainly means that something new, even for God, comes into existence, in that creation begins which was not before. But it also implies, again as Athanasius continues, the Word comes to be what he was not before:

> Therefore the creatures began to be made; but the Word of God, not having beginning of being, certainly did not begin to be, nor begin to come to be, but was ever. And the works have their beginning in their making, and their beginning precedes their coming to be; but the Word, not being of things which come to be, rather comes to be the Framer of those which have a beginning.

That is to say: behind the creation itself, with its beginning, there is a transcendent beginning in the Being of God who, as Triune Being, is without beginning. It is precisely this which gives such amazing profundity to the concept of *creatio ex nihilo*, creation out of nothing.

To say that there is a 'beginning' in God is not to suggest, by the application of the term, that God does not remain eternally the God he is. But it does speak of a freedom within the Godhead to do, in accordance with what he eternally is, what he had not done 'previously'. Yet this freedom must be instantaneous with what he eternally is, otherwise temporal measurement is inflicted upon the Being of God.

Here the limitation of language again rears up. The very use of 'instantaneous', itself a temporal term, is inadequate. It can only be used as a pointer and a suggestion, taken from our refracted existence to speak of the singularity of God which must always confront us as mystery.

Basil in his *Hexaermeron* I:5-6, gathers up much of the same sort of argument, though it is couched in terms of the invisible world rather than the creation in the mind of God. This is quoted quite fully as it is an insight into a Patristic commenting mind concerning the concept of *beginning*.

> It appears, indeed, that even before this world an order of things existed, of which our minds can form an idea, but of which we can say nothing, because it is too lofty a subject for men who are but beginners and babes in knowledge. The birth of the world was preceded by a condition of things suitable for the exercise of supernatural powers, outstripping the limits of time, eternal and infinite. The Creator . . . of the universe perfected His works on it, spiritual light for the happiness of all who love the Lord, intellectual and invisible natures, all the orderly arrangement of pure intelligences who are beyond the reach of our mind and of whom we cannot even discover the names. They fill the essence of this invisible world, as Paul teaches us. 'For by Him were all things created that are in heaven, and that are in earth, visible and invisible whether they be thrones or dominions or principalities or powers' or virtues or hosts of angels or the dignities of archangels. To this world at last it was necessary to add a new world, both a school and a training place where the souls of men should be taught and a home for beings destined to be born and to die. Thus was created, of a nature analogous to this world and the animals and plants which live thereon, the succession of time, for ever pressing on and passing away and never stopping in its course. Is not this the nature of time, where the past is no more, the future does not exist, and the present escapes before being recognised? And such also is the nature of the creature which lives in time, – condemned to grow or perish without rest and without certain stability. It is therefore fit that the bodies of animals and plants, obliged to follow a sort of current, and carried away by the motion which leads them to birth or to death, should

live in the midst of surroundings whose nature is in accord with beings subject to change. Thus the writer who wisely tells us of the birth of the Universe does not fail to put these words at the head of the narrative 'In the beginning God created'; that is to say, in the beginning of time. Therefore if He makes the world appear in the beginning, it is not a proof that its birth has preceded all other things that were made. He only wishes to tell us that, after the invisible and intellectual world, the visible world, the world of the senses, began to exist. The first movement is called beginning. 'To do right is the beginning of the good way'. Just actions are truly the first step towards a happy life. Again, we call 'beginning' the essential and first part from which a thing proceeds, such as the foundation of a house, the keel of a vessel; it is in this sense that it is said 'The fear of the Lord is the beginning of wisdom', that is to say that piety is, as it were, the groundwork and foundation of perfection. Art is also the beginning of the works of artists, the skill of Bezaleel began the adornment of the tabernacle. Often even the good which is the final cause is the beginning of actions. Thus the approbation of God is the beginning of almsgiving, and the end laid up for us in the promises the beginning of all virtuous efforts.

Such being the different senses of the word beginning, see if we have not all the meanings here. You may know the epoch when the formation of this world began, if, ascending into the past, you endeavour to discover the first day. You will thus find what was the first movement of time; then that the creation of the heavens and earth were like the groundwork, and afterwards that an intelligent reason, as the word beginning indicates, presided in the order of visible things. You will finally discover that the world was not conceived by chance and without reason, but for an useful end and for the great advantage of all beings, since it is really the school where reasonable souls exercise themselves, the training ground where they learn to know God; since by the sight of visible and sensible things, the mind is led, as by a hand, to the contemplation of invisible things. 'For', as the Apostle says, 'the invisible things of Him from the creation of the world are clearly seen, being understood by the things that are made'. Perhaps these words 'In the beginning God created' signify the rapid and imperceptible moment of creation. The beginning, in effect, is indivisible and instantaneous. The beginning of the road is not yet the road, and that of the house is not yet the house; so the beginning of time is not yet time, and not even the least particle of it. If some objector tell us that the beginning is a time, he ought then, as he knows well, to submit it to the division of time – a beginning, a middle and an end. Now it is ridiculous to imagine a beginning of a beginning. Further, if we divide the beginning into two, we make two instead of one, or rather make several; we

really make an infinity, for all that which is divided is divisible to
the infinite. Thus, then if it is said, 'In the beginning God
created', it is to teach us that in the will of God the world arose in
less than an instant, and it is to convey this meaning more clearly
that other interpreters have said: 'God made summarily' that is to
say, all at once and in a moment. But enough concerning the
beginning, if only to put a few points out of many.

These explorations by Basil into the meaning of 'beginning',
fascinated Grosseteste, and inspired him to look into the matter
in his own way[4]. While using Basil as his fundamental inspiration
and guide, he adds much by way of additional interpretation. He
outlines many examples of the meaning of *beginning* drawn from
biblical narratives and philosophical observations. Having done
this, he ends:[5]

> *Tot igitur modis, et forte aliquibus qui me latent aliis, dicto 'principio'
> creavit Deus celum et terram 'in principio'.*

> In all these, and perhaps in other ways which are hidden from
> me, these words 'In the beginning' show how God created heaven
> and earth in the beginning.

Based on Basil, Grosseteste's developed argument here is the
insistence that *beginning* and all the considerations which stem
from this word, are not to be construed in temporal terms but by
way of the relations between Creator and created time and space.
The word is to be interpreted in terms of contingency to and
from God who is uncreated and not measurable (even infinitely
so) spatially or temporally.

Clearly this involves a careful consideration of terminology
and verbal images when speaking about God and eternity. We
have already noted[6] Grosseteste's insistence in his *Commentary
on the Celestial Hierarchies* that all verbal images were to be
cleansed of their material content, creaturely implications, and
temporal and spatial meanings, when applied to God. This is
absolutely necessary when we examine the implications of
beginning.

That there should be a beginning involves God as Creator. It
is his creation which has a beginning. But this is not some
happen chance event. It is his deliberate and considered intent,
decree and design. How then does this beginning stand in
relation to Him? Here our language breaks down and we have to
tread circumspectly and be aware of our terms. If this beginning is

not 'new' for God, then the 'beginning' of creation must be the same as the 'beginning' of God. They would be co-terminous, and we have posited an idea of the eternity of the world. In other words there is no beginning of creation whatsoever.

The very word – as Basil and Grosseteste and all Hexaemeronic commentators indicate in one degree or another – demands that we say that it is that which God begins. Yet we cannot speak of a 'before' the beginning, as though God existed in time, however infinite. Nor does the employment of the world 'timelessness' help here with regard to the existence of God. It is an unwarranted and meaningless gloss on the term 'eternity', which is really only a term of convenience indicating that which we cannot grasp which is beyond time and not of its quality – unless, of course, we think of eternity as endless time, which makes God qualitatively no different from us in our short temporal existence.

In any case, time and space being inseparably bound, if God exists in endless time, he must also be of endless size! But 'size' is meaningless if it is endless and immeasurable; the very word presupposes limitations. So it is with 'time'. Such reasoning is entirely unproductive. We could go on, and on, and on, speculating and projecting as another dimension what Dunne called *three dimensional instabilities.* Indeed we are at danger of projecting that other false dimension precisely because of these instabilities with which we cannot cope.[7] We are projecting the creaturely content of our thinking, and elevating it to what we call God. The God we have so named is but that which we know from our existence, but to the Nth degree.

But let us assume God.

We are faced with having to say that there is a beginning for God. But this beginning is not merely the *beginning* of the creation narrative. Here again all care has to be exercised, for it was precisely on the point of ἀρχή, this *beginning* for God, that Arianism foundered in its interpretation, having, one must suspect, posed the same question. The Arian solution was to give the Word of God as Creator a beginning within the created dimension. In this they misinterpreted the text describing the Word as *the first-born of every creature*[8] – that is, they saw this as meaning that he was the first thing created by God, when the text within its context clearly refers to the headship of all created things.

Athanasius faced the same sort of problems against the Arians, and we may consider here a resumé of some of what he says. He clearly asserts, again and again, that there is a beginning for God. But he does so having carefully considered the way we speak in such terms. He is insistent that there can be no disjunction between nature – that is, what things are in themselves as they really are in themselves – and truth – that is, the truth that we express about that objective reality of these things.

But obviously there is a disjunction. We can only talk and formulate expressions, out of this world of time and things. How are we to employ language and terms that are appropriate to whatever, as it is in itself, may be beyond this world? How can we know what lies beyond this 'present' age, unless that has some relation to our dimension, and has given us something of its nature to grasp? In other words, how can we speak of this beyond unless it permits us to do so out of its own nature and in a way consistent with what it is in itself?

That is where there is an equal insistence on the fact that we can only know God in his self-revelation, that all thinking and speaking about God has to be undertaken from that centre which is Jesus Christ. For what God is eternally in himself, he is the same towards us in Christ. It is here that the disjunction fades, not because we have discovered for ourselves the nature of what lies beyond this world and have formulated an appropriate terminology to describe its truth, but because that which lies beyond has arisen out of that beyond and come into the here and now without compromising its essential nature.

But within this God-overruled disjunction, there is a necessary disjunction in the matter of our part in response to this personal action of God. We have to distinguish between truth itself and our statements about it. We cannot think to contain and adequately speak about this revelation of God, even if it takes place within the dimension of time and things. It is still God who confront us in this unique action and event of Jesus Christ. The truth of that is, and remains, whatever we may say about it. The truth of that is the primary factor and calls forth out of what it is in itself statements from us appropriate to its nature. It is not on the same level as, and competing on equal terms with, other truths which are merely of this dimension of time and space. It is an event of the eternal Word or Son of God, one with the Father and the Holy Spirit, who, while taking our flesh and nature to himself and giving it existence in union with himself, remains God. It is truth cut in from outside this dimension.

The truth about anything is that which cannot be other than what that object really is. The truth about anything is entirely and utterly consistent with the nature of that object. This we may call its *inner integrity*, for truth and nature repose in perfect harmony in any particular object. But that object discloses itself to us as it is in itself. It reveals itself to be exactly what it is. This we may call its *outer integrity*. When this is applied to the revelation of God in Christ, we find, again, that what God eternally is in himself, he is towards us in Christ. There is no gulf, contradiction or disjunction between what God is and what he is in his revelation to us.

We have to be aware of the relationship of truth with truthfulness. Truthfulness is openness to the truth. Right reasoning means that the mind is orientated to the nature of the object – that object in its self-truth – which it is studying. It will not approach that object with preconceptions about it, or seek to fit it into a framework of theory which it has already deduced from other sources. Such is the hallmark of objective reasoning and therefore of truthfulness.

But our truthfulness is utterly dependent on the truth itself. The object of any study will remain what it was before we began to study it, will remain what it is as we study it, and remain what it is whatever the results we seek to claim about it. It is not changed by our representation or misrepresentation of it. Even despite us it retains its essential integrity. Its priority over our minds will be acknowledged when we are truthful about it. For it will be seen that it is the object itself in its self integrity which has caused our perceiving of it, compelled our receiving of it, and remains the totally sufficient and only source of our conceiving it to be what it is. It is known only on the grounds of its own authority. When we say 'an authoritative statement concerning the truth', the authority in fact rests in the truth and not in the statement as such. That is why we have to distinguish between truth itself and our statements about it. Truthfulness and statements about truth serve the truth; they are not dominant over it.

Theology is the attempt to make our statements compatible with the nature of the revelation of God, or rather, to make them appropriate pointers to it, while always giving it priority over them. Theology is therefore a matter of constant reformation of thought and concepts about revelation, for these concepts and statements have to be constantly re-examined in the light of that revelation, submitting to the compelling majesty of its unsurrendered integrity. God may give himself to us in revelation, but he does not give himself up to us. At the very point where he seems to have surrendered and given himself up, the Crucifixion itself, his Lordship and Priority is asserted in Resurrection and Ascension. The 'how' of God, the 'how' God has acted in revelation, in Incarnation, Crucifixion, Resurrection and Ascension, must ever remain beyond our grasp.

But here in his self-revelation, we are given the entrance into the very eternal Being of God who comes to us on his own terms. Bearing in mind the essential impropriety of our concepts and statements about him, we are nevertheless compelled and enabled to make them as appropriate as possible within our limitations. All theology is therefore essentially Christologically paradeigmatic. On that basis it is concerned with openness to the truth and letting God's terms be heard and seen in this self-revelation, and not darkened and dulled by any unwarranted and irrational human intrusions of thought, however high and laudable these may be.

Thus when we talk of a *beginning*, we must refer in the first instance, as the determinative norm, to Christ himself. It was to this norm that Athanasius turned in his dispute with the Arians in the fourth century over the question of the interpretation of *beginning*. He took the text which the Arians were fond of quoting, Proverbs VIII:22 in the Septuagint version:

> The Lord created me a beginning [ἀρχή) of his ways for His works.

Christ had been identified with the Wisdom of God, the *me* of this text, by the early Church in its theological thinking. To the Arians this was a statement that the Word, or Wisdom of God was a created Being, the first of all creatures with pre-eminence over all other created things. Athanasius countered this by insisting that, in His human nature, Jesus Christ had been created by God as the Beginning of all his ways and works towards creation. He, *in his humanity*, was the Archetype of all creation.

Athanasius brings together[9] the Incarnation of the Word and the creation of humanity.

For if, out of a former normal state of non-existence, they were called into being by the Presence and loving kindness of the Word, it followed naturally that when men were bereft of the knowledge of God and were turned back to what was not (for evil is what is not, and what is good is), they should, since they derive their being from God Who IS, be everlasting bereft even of being; in other words that they should be disintegrated and abide in death and corruption . . .

For God has not only made us out of nothing; but He gave us freely, by the grace of the Word, a life in correspondence with God. But men, having rejected things eternal, . . . became the cause of their own corruption in death, being . . . by nature corruptible, but destined, by the grace following from partaking of the Word, to have escaped their natural state . . . For because of the Word dwelling with them, even their natural corruption did not come near them, as Wisdom also says: 'God made man for incorruption, and as an image of His own eternity, but by envy of the devil death came into the world'.

There are several considerations here in Athanasius's thought. The first to note is that of contingency to and from God. Humanity is called into being out of nothing, and depends upon God for the sustenance of its true creative intent – *a life in correspondence to God*. This is contingency TO God.

Yet humanity has its own dimension and identity. It is given a life an identity and a purpose *freely* – and this is contingency FROM God.

But the principle of this double contingency is the Word, by whom all things are made.

The second consideration is that of the implied effect of time. Held in the proper contingent relation to God through the Word, there is no decay or change. Therefore time does not exert that change whereby humanity moves to its equilibrium in death. In that relation, the equilibrium is the grace of the Word in which man finds his nature in the creative intent of God.

The third consideration is that this relation is in the creative intent and purpose of God, of which, according to Athanasius and Irenaeus, the Word is the Beginning and the Archetype. Indeed, the Word is this relation for all that is brought into being out of nothing.

But what does this mean for God who brings something into being in contingent relation with himself which was not 'before' he so created it? Here I wish to turn to the later works of Robert

Grosseteste, for there we find that much of what has already been put forward is heightened in his considerations of light as the beginning of creation, and of light created in its relation to God as uncreated Light.

LIGHT: THE BEGINNING

We cannot avoid the fact that for the mediaeval mind, angels are an important factor in any discussion of creation, and particularly in the question of the *beginning*. We can take it, however, that this emphasis is but the fashion of the theology of the age in penetrating into the mysteries of the creative act of God. In a sense, angelology for Grosseteste is a secondary feature of little independent import, save where the subject of angels is used as a clarification of the question of the place of light and understanding in creation.

It is because of this juxtaposition of angels, light and knowledge that we have to take into account the place of angelology in Grosseteste's thinking. His angelology is set out for the most part in his little treatise *De Intelligentiis*, the second part of a long letter addressed to Master Adam Rufus who had posed questions to him. There is little here for our particular consideration, since it deals with angels as messengers and ministers of God, and not their significance for Grosseteste's mind in relation to creation and light. But even here, using a quotation from Augustine,[10] he warns against projecting material thoughts into things spiritual, conceiving such in 'sensuous' images.

In one of his *Charges to the Clergy*[11] we begin to perceive the part that angels played in Grosseteste's view of creation and light. This sets out their relationship to God as determinative of their status and function. Here, angels are regarded as pure, intellectual substances, whose singular function of intelligence is fixed solely on the contemplation of the Trinity. The Word is their mirror and their book, in whom they see eternity and life, and the majesty, might, wisdom and grace of God. All that they are in their existence, contemplation, adoration and action, is a singular and simple expression of spiritual light, such as humanity should long for but, though capable of achieving it, yet must seek it even within its limitations and weakness.

The exemplarity of angels as created spiritual light contemplat-

ing and adoring and thus sharing in uncreated Light, is best set
out in the *Hexaemeron*. Here [12] Grosseteste claims that angels are
not excluded from the creation narrative. In the very creation of
light their creation is contained. They are reflections of the first
light, for they are pure intelligences, intellectual beings of sheer
enlightenment.

Light is the purest form of matter. In the symbolism of
Genesis, both the creation of angels and the ground and form of
all created things is light itself. Light is inextricably woven to the
concept of order; indeed, light is order and order is light. Light is
seen in the first instance as that which is uncreated Light, the
order which God eternally is in himself as Father, Son bound in
the bond of eternal Love, the Holy Spirit. This uncreated Light
is reflected in the created light, which is the form and the quality
most approximate to that which God is as uncreated Light. This
created light manifests itself throughout the orders of angels,
down through all the created orders of the heavens and the earth.
It is the unifying factor of all creation, heavenly and earthly,
spiritual and material, and as that factor, that which is supremely
contingent to and from the uncreated Light of God himself.

In positing a particular angelology in which angels, created
with the creation of light the first form of all creation, are
regarded as transcending this gulf in their very being, and by
insisting generally on a twofold noetic and ontic role of light as the
ground of all created being in form and matter, both spiritual
and material, Grosseteste removes himself from all the then
prevailing dichotomies in mediaeval thought between these
categories. As that which pervades and characterises all creation,
heavenly and earthly, light transcends any dualistic gulf, and is
both the unifying factor of all creation and the principium of
contingency to and from God

By *spiritual* Grossteste means above all *Intellectual* or *Intelligent
being* – intellectual and intelligent, referring not to cleverness, but
to that which is in such a relation to God that its understanding
and existence is formed by the sheer bond of its contingency to,
and the nearness of its obedient contingency from, him. That is
why though humanity is of flesh and blood it nevertheless within
the limits of this condition is to realize that it is 'spiritual' in this
sense.

This is best illustrated by Grosetteste's insistence on the
goodness of material things and in their function. His view of

sexual matters and sexual function, for example, (that area where
mediaeval puritanism engendered by dualistic reasoning was at
its most severe), runs counter to the tenor of his times.[13]

> The body of a man is better and nobler than any tree; and that of
> a woman nobler than the earth. And the seed from the man's
> body from which a man is generated is better and nobler than any
> other kind of sowing. Therefore the seed from the body of a man
> falling into the body of a woman to procreate children is –
> barring the defilement of carnal concupiscence – better and
> nobler than any kind of seed falling into the ground. Conse-
> quently, good, pure and honest meditation on this is better and
> more honorable than meditation on the procreation of trees,
> provided it is not contaminated by concupiscence or corruption.
> And the same may be said about the organs of generation, which
> are not to be thought shameful.

His was a unitary, as opposed to the prevailing dualistic, way
of thinking. And this way of thinking is based on the status and
role of light in its relation to uncreated Light. This is clear from
his observation on the senses, which he divides into external and
internal. Of the external, sight is the prime sense, and by nature,
different from the other four, because light is both the object
which gives the ability to see, and that which enlightens what is
seen.

There is an order and a gradation of the senses, for they are
linked to an order and gradation of the things for which they
were created. Hearing, smell, taste and touch, all are graded
according to the heaviness, or thickness of the element concerned.
Hearing comes from the higher, finer air; smell from the thicker,
lower air; taste from water activity; touch from material itself.
But all these are bonded together in their respective places in this
descending order, by light in its descent to the gross elements in
which its activity is weaker the lower the element, but nevertheless active.

This distribution of matter in more and more solid quantity, is
explained in *De Luce*. At creation, light, created as a simple
point, expands *infinitely* (in our calculation). This expansion
spreads matter spherically, equally in every direction, such is the
movement of light, from that simple point of no dimension.
Expanding by sphere upon sphere (nine heavenly and four lower
in all, according to Grosseteste, following the then generally
accepted Patristic observances) each of the nine spheres is quali-

fied by the action of lux propagating *lumen*, light begetting light, and light begotten by light – a derivative process. But because it is derivative, the process is characterized by increasing weakness, which results in increasing density and loss of purity owing to the diminishing power of lumen from sphere to sphere. Light is simpler and more 'spiritual' in the higher and heavenly spheres, more diverse and corporeal in the lower.

Here we have a whole hierarchy of order and quality, but all contained in the simplicity and singularity of the first light which moves out to the furthest reaches equally in every direction, then inwards, sphere upon sphere by its generated *lumen* – the inner circumference of the higher sphere simultaneous with the outer circumference of the lower. The unity of all is contained in that first light, as indeed is all that is. All things, it may be concluded, are present in that initial, simple singularity of light, the first created form and corporeity itself. It is the unity of all things in their diversity, their order and their harmony, and the totality of their existence. It is recapitulation in reverse – all things first contained in the simple point of light at its creation, and then spread into their places according to their quality and nature determined by the quality, nature and activity of light.

So it is with the inward or internal senses. They are a *sensus communis*, that is, they are profoundly related through light, having their origin and grounding in that light. They give intelligibility to the perception of the external senses, and come together with all data in a unity of light-engendered cognition and interpretation.

Thus light is the *principium unitatis* of all things, bestowing rationality and order, pervading and adorning the confronting object and the knowing subject, giving order and intelligibility externally and internally. In *De Luce*, Grosseteste describes light as *species et perfectio corporum omnium* – the glory and perfection of all embodied things.

But light is indivisible – both spatially and temporarily. Here we must concern ourselves with the nature of created light at creation itself, and what Grosseteste's angelology has to add in the understanding of this.

We need not concern ourselves with his comments on the hierarchies of angels and heavenly powers, for which he is clearly dependent on (with some variations) the work of Pseudo-Dionysius. The only area concerning us here is his insistence on harmony and order in the hierarchical placement of angelic beings.

What is pertinent and of import is the conjunction of angels and the 'days' of creation as recounted in Genesis. The angels enjoy undiminishing contemplation and uninterrupted clarity of the vision of God. It is this privileged sight which gives them their place in the creative act of God.

The danger exhibited in the works of some mediaeval writers on the subject is that the angels are described in terms of being mediators, and, in some instances agents, in the work of creation. This may well be the influence of those Arabic commentators on cosmology – Averroes (Ibn Rushd), Avicerbrol (Solomon Ibn Gebirol) and Avincenna (Ibn Sina) – to whom the west, in the twelfth and thirteenth centuries looked for their valued commentaries on the classical Greek philosophers. While Grosseteste had recourse to these, and his use of them is clear, he would have none of this.

Although angels have pre-eminence of being, being pure spirit, they are created beings, whatever pre-eminence in the orders of creation they enjoy. And they are created not to be co-creators with God. There is a decisive qualitative difference between Creator and created. There is no blurring of the edges by introducing emanations from God in a descending scale to present, in the fashion of dualistic thought, a protection for God against being tainted with having anything to do with matter.

Rather, as has been stressed above, the angels are exemplary in their contemplation of God and the acts of God. They are ideals whose state it is impossible for humanity to achieve but towards such like it nevertheless must seek to strive within its grosser limitations.

It is their relation to light which is the key to unlock the answer to their import vis-a-vis God and the rest of creation. Indeed much of what may be said of light may be said of the angelic state and function. I suspect that Grosseteste unwittingly relates them to time, for they are concerned with the movement and action of light, as well as so closely participating in its nature and quality.

This train of thought is set out in his *De Cessatione Legalium*, and in the *Commentary on the Posterior Analytics*, but most profoundly in the *Hexaemeron*. It is in the last that the role of angels in the creative act of God is stressed. In *De Cessatione Legalium*, Grosseteste clearly asserts the simultaneity of all creation on the basis of the text of Ecclesiasticus, chapter 18, verse 1 – (McEvoy notes this reference as being from Wisdom, which commonly refers to the book entitled 'The Wisdom of Solomon', while he is really referring to 'The Wisdom of Jesus the Son of Sirach', commonly called 'Ecclesiasticus'.)

> *Qui vivit in aeternum creavit omnia simul.*

> He who lives eternally created all things simultaneously

He develops this in the *Hexaemeron*, questioning why Augustine is less decisive in the matter than Jerome and Basil who state the simultaneity of all creation clearly.[14] He certainly uses Augustine's work[15] as part basis for his development of the simultaneity of creation and the place of angels in this act of God. However, the question must be asked if Grosseteste is not also and more so, dependent on John Philoponos, the sixth century Alexandrian thinker. He neither makes mention of the name nor acknowledges any source for his statements, but the parellelism of thought is remarkable. The particular point of remark is that Grosseteste looks, certainly as Augustine did, on the relation between angels and days in the Genesis narrative. But while Augustine[16] identifies the angels with the days of creation (days being light and angels light also) Grosseteste sees this relation in a far more involved and intriguing way in terms of the simultaneity of creation.

Augustine describes the days of creation as the cognition of the orders of creation within the angelic mind. As pure intelligences, the angels perceive the development of creation as unfolding in sequence, though the cycle of each day and the events therein are, in temporal terms, simultaneous. The first day consists of the angel's knowledge of itself, the second of the firmament, and then on through the rest of the created orders including the creation of humanity on the sixth day. The 'days' are characterised not by time, in our sense, but by the threefold process of cognition set out in terms of the brightest light (mid-day), the dimmest light (evening) and the dawning light (morning). The brightest light is the angelic perception of the particular order of creation seen in the decree of the eternal Word; the dimmest light the cognition of that order realized and made by the Word; and the dawning light the perception of the relation of the

particular order to the Word by Whom it was created, that is, its
contingency to and from the Word.

The problem left by Augustine is typified by his statement[17]
that

> Time does not exist without some movement and transition . . .
> Then assuredly the world was made not in time, but simultane-
> ously with time. For that which is made in time is made both
> after and before some time – after that which is past, before that
> which is future. But none could then be past, for there was no
> creature by whose movement its duration could be measured. But
> simultaneously with time the world was made, if in the world's
> creation change and motion were created as seems evident from
> the order of the first six or seven days.

There is an unresolved ambiguity here, caused by the particular
use of *change* and *motion* in conjunction with *time*, so that
although the simultaneity of creation is stressed, nevertheless the
creation is seen as a successive temporal unfolding of moments
simultaneous in each day only.

While Grosseteste follows this, he deals more determinedly
and firmly with what is left untied together untidily by Augustine, namely the question of the simultaneity of the whole process of creation, the apparent sequence of 'days' and what is
meant by *change* and *motion* in the act of creation. This he does
by his exposition of the angelic cognition of creation and its
orders.[18] Not only in the sequence of each 'day', but in the
totality of the 'days' of creation is there simultaneity. Moreover,
and most importantly, angels, for Grosseteste, transcend time,
or rather, bore a superior relation to all time. This development
runs clearly throughout those passages dealing with angelology
in the *Hexaemeron*. This relation can only be if all time is
recapitulate in that Primordial Point of light, that singularity
of creation. Change and motion are in relation to recapitulative
time.

The first day's creation of light is not only of light itself but of
being-in-light and being-of-light – the creation of the angelic
existence. The cycle of brightness, dimmer light and dawn light
consists of the angel's cognition of its being in the Divine mind
and decree, the knowledge of itself which (it being less than the
Divine) means that this dimmer light corresponds to the awareness of the angel in realizing its difference from and dependence
on God – its contingency to and from God in his creative love

and grace – and finally the dawn light of its contemplation of its being and role in relation to the Triune existence of the eternal Creator. So too, on the second day, the creation of the firmament, the angelic cognition perceives it in the Divine mind, as actualized and in its relation to the Creator.

The development of Grosseteste from Augustine is that the whole creation process is simultaneous. The days are cyclical cognitions embracing the fulness of the act of creation, from the Divine decree through the actualisation of the decree to the recognition of the relation of the finished work in its contingent relation to God. He describes this cyclical process of 'days' in the angelic intelligence.[19]

> *Item vespere et mane aliter intelliguntur. Prima namque lux, ut dictum est, secundum Augustinum est angelica natura ad Deum conversa, et conversione que ad Deum est deiformis effecta. In qua deiformitate ipsa est quasi lux et dies, post tenebras negacionis existencie sue et post tenebras privacionis in se naturaliter precedentis hanc lucem sue deiformitatis, que erant quasi tenebre super faciem abyssi. In hac vero luce et die cognovit Creatorem, et se ipsam in racione sua creatrice in mente divina. Huius itaque prime diei vespera est, post lucem dicte cognicionis, velud obscurior cognicio sue proprie nature in se, qua cognoscit quod ipsa non est hoc quod Deus. Cum vero, post hanc obscuriorem cognicionem sui in se, refert se ad laudandam ipsam lucem que Deus est, cuius contemplacione formatur, et percipit in ipsa luce firmamentum creandum, fit mane, finiens velud primum diem naturalem et velud inchoans secundum diem.*

Likewise 'the evening and the morning' are interpreted differently. For the first light, as we are told, is, according to Augustine, the angelic nature turned towards God, and by this turning which is towards God, it is made deiform. In this God-like form it is in itself like light and day, after the darkness of the negation of its own existence and after the darkness of privation in itself, coming naturally before this light of its God-like form, which was like the darkness on the face of the deep. Indeed in this light and day it recognized the Creator, and recognized its own reason for creation in the divine mind. And so of this first day there is an evening, after the light of the aforesaid recognition, like a darker recognition of its own nature in itself, by which it recognizes that it is not in itself that which God (is). When indeed after this darker recognition of itself in itself, it returns to praising the light which God is, by the contemplation of whom it is formed and it perceives in the light itself the creation of the firmament, (as though) it were morning, as though finishing the first natural day and as though beginning the second day.

Grosseteste's thought concerning the cyclical nature of the angel's contemplation can be summarized thus: When God says *Let there be, fiat*, the angel perceives the reason for that particular creation lodged in the eternal Word; *and so it was made, et sic est factum*, refers to the cognizance of that creation impressed on the angelic intelligence; the statement *it was so* (here *quod fecit deus*) points to the affirmation of the angel of the actuality of that creation in its tangible being. But, as there can be no intrusion of temporal values into the eternity of God, there is no time lapse between the decree, the deed and the accomplishment. The will and the act and the deed are 'instantaneous'. And this is for all the 'days' of creation; the six are but qualitative distinctions instantly accomplished.

The simultaneous cyclical cognitions, graded by light, in the angelic mind concerning all the simultaneous 'days' of creation, are accomplished in a twinkling. He illustrates this[20] by pointing out that the sun's light going through a transparent material illuminates all of it simultaneously, but those parts nearer the light more clearly.

> ... *quemadmodum solis splendor subito pertransit et simul tempore illustrat loca soli viciniora et remociora cum tamen prius natura illustret loca proximiora.*

> ... just as for instance the brightness of the sun passes through suddenly and lights up the places closer to and the parts more distant from the sun simultaneously, although however nature lights the nearest places most clearly.

What this illustration does is to show that the demarcation into 'days' in the Genesis narrative, is not regarded by Grosseteste as a temporal division, but a division of quality determined by light. This corresponds to the statements about noonday, evening and morning light; they refer respectively to the quality perceived by the angelic mind – first the splendour of uncreated Light, God himself, then the angel's lesser created being in itself, and last the wonder of that being in the contingent relation of grace and love to its Creator.

In the same way, all the 'days' are as one, diversified only by the quality of what is perceived – on the first the pure light and angelic being, on the second the firmament, and so on until the sixth day. But the cycle of the second day is the same cycle as the first. It is differentiated not by time but by the perception of the particular order of creation concerned. And so with all the days. All the orders of creation are simultaneously perceived at the *beginning* – at that first act of creation, the bringing into existence of light in a twinkling, and contained within it.

It is the business of the angelic creation to bring creation's praise throughout the orders of creation in their diversity, before the throne of the Creator. In this respect we may see a parallel between the angels as creatures of the first light, and therefore supremely rational beings, and humanity, as the last and crown of God's creation, which, with its rational mind also praises God itself for its own being and appointment and also on behalf of all else over which, in the corporeal world, it has been given dominion and responsibility. At the 'beginning' and 'end' of creation, we have the creation of rational beings, the one heavenly, the other earthy, encompassing the work of God.

It is necessary to point out that while some of the statements employed by Grosseteste would seem to suggest that he had either fallen into a general tendency of gnosticism with regard to creation, or that he was claiming the employment of particular intermediaries by God in the work of creation, he expressly repudiates such views in the *Hexaemeron*. He denounces the views of Plato regarding a Demiurge who employed demigods to create matter, keeping the creation of things spiritual to himself; the 'Jewish fable' that God conversed with the angels in making man (hence 'in our image' was interpreted as that of God and the angels); and those attitudes which may well be those of the Arabic commentators following a Neo-Platonic emphasis developed from Plato himself. Grosseteste is clear, and expresses himself in no uncertain terms on the matter that the eternal Word is the eternal Son, God of God, by whom alone the Father made all things in the bond of the Spirit – that creation is solely the work of the Triune God. The following[21] is typical of Grosseteste's linking of the all-sufficient Trinity and the work of creation:

> *Dixit itaque Deus, hoc est: Verbum sibi coeternum genuit. Diccio enim Verbi est generacio, et cum alius si qui gignit et alius qui gignitur, habes hic duas personas, patris videlicit et Filii, patenter expressas; et in superioribus expressus fuit Dei spiritus. Unde iam tota Trinitas expressa est; bis videlicet Pater et Filius; semel cum dictum est supra In principio fecit Deus, et iterum cum dictum est nunc Dixit Deus; et semel Spiritus Sanctus, cum dictum est: Spiritus Domini ferebatur super aquas.*

'And so God said': that is to say, He begat the Word co-eternal with Himself. For the saying of the Word is its begetting, and when one begets and another is begotten, you have here two persons, those of the Father and the Son, made manifest plainly; and the Spirit of God was made manifest earlier [in the text]. From whence it is the whole Trinity now made manifest; the Father and the Son twice – once when it was said above 'In the beginning God created', and again when it is now said 'God said'; and the Holy Spirit once, when it was said 'The Spirit of the Lord was borne upon the waters'.

The Trinity is all sufficient and acts solely in that sufficiency. The role of the angels is not that of active mediators in the work of creation; they are ministers and servants, διάκονοι, whose function is to understand the creative intent of the Triune God for all creation in its respective orders (including themselves) and to gather up all adoration, praise and thanksgiving for the wonders they behold. They are witnesses to the love and grace and order of the Trinity in creating immediately in the first twinkling of light all that is. In this way, light, illumination, grace and love and order are beheld and gathered up in the one instant angelic proclamation of creation before God.

This means that not only all things which exist are brought into being in their fulness and completion at that instant of creation which defies temporal measurement, but also all time, which to us is divided into a past, a present and a future, is there in all its fulness and completion, for God in that indescribable instant of his creation of light.

The *beginning* now also refers to the *completeness* – that is to the end or the fulfilment. It is all contained in that first light. Here, of course, we are back in the realm of Christological debate concerning the Word as that light referred to in St John's Gospel, and to His work, in Irenaean terms, of *joining the end to the beginning*. The Word is uncreated Light, but as the works of God correspond to his Being in their created character, so too created light corresponds to uncreated light. This *beginning* of light, and of all time and things, encompassing in it the fulness of all time and things, corresponds to that which is a *beginning* for God in his Being. There is, in other words a correspondence between the *beginning* for created time and light, and a *beginning* for God in uncreated Time as uncreated Light.

This *beginning* in the uncreated Time of God (commonly

called his 'eternity'), centres on the eternal Word, for while the Father is eternally the Father of the Son, he was not always Creator, and while the Son is eternally the Son of the Father, he was not always the Creator by whom all things were made. This is not, it must be repeated, a projection of time values into the uncreated Time of God, but, in the limitations of our language bound by time, a pointer to the fact that God takes another quality to himself within the freedom of his all-sufficiency, and decrees that he 'will be' also Creator, and the Son 'will be' the One by whom all things are created.

It is necessary to clarify this, for it is part of the very fine point which divided the Arians from the orthodox in the fourth century – which dispute resulted in the Nicene Creed of AD 325, and its subsequent enlargement in AD 381 at the Council of Constantinople to the form now received and repeated. The crucial debate with the Arians behind these Councils was the difference between the eternal begetting of the Son or Word by the Father, and the creation of all things. The one is internal to the eternal life of the Trinity and of the nature of God, the latter is external to the interior life of God and is by his will. The Arian confusion was to identify the generation of the Word with the act of creation. The Son eternally co-exists with the Father and the Spirit; creation has a beginning out of nothing.[22] For God to beget is primary; for him to create is secondary.[23]

When therefore, it must be emphasised, we speak of a *beginning* in the eternal life of God, or a *new beginning*, we must beware of projecting the content of our time-related language, temporal concepts into the Being of God. Gregory Nazianzen speaks clearly of this:[24]

> God always was and always is; or rather, God always is. For was and will be are fragments of our time, and are of changeable nature, but He is eternal being.

This *beginning* can only be construed in terms of God's freedom, which is not an arbitrary freedom, but one consistent with the God he eternally is, that is, a God of love. He exists in Divine Order, as the Father and Son bound in the eternal bond of Love, the Holy Spirit. It is an existence of Love and Order. The Incarnation reveals that God is free to become what he 'was' not 'before', that is, to take human nature and flesh to himself in union and give it existence as the man Jesus within that union.

In the same way, he is free to become, in his eternal existence, Creator as well as Father of the Son and Son of the Father.

The question is: Does God find that he has to have two *beginnings* – creation and incarnation, or are these but two facets of the one *beginning*?

5

The Individual and Time

GOD DOES not exist in time. That is not to say that he does not have a relation to time; it is to say that he is not circumscribed by a span of time, nor is his Being conditioned by the passage of time. We, on the other hand, are bound by time and utterly characterised by its passing.

Strictly speaking we are characterised by the direction of the passage of time, that is, as it moves towards the future throwing up our past in the process. However, this direction of time is by no means easy to prove in scientific terms. 'Living in the past' is, for some persons, more than just a recall of memory, as is 'hoping in the future' for some more than mere optimism. Both can, for those who for one reason or another cannot cope, be ways of life. And even for those who can be regarded as sane and sufficient, if due thought is given to the insubstantiality and indescribability of what is conveniently called 'past', 'present' and 'future' – which dilemma we have already noted[1] – the elusiveness of time considered by itself is inconclusive of any confidence in the matter of time's direction. We can only say that commonsense tells us that we have a past, a present (however incalculably infinitesimal) and at least the hope of a future. But beyond the level of the awareness of commonsense, proof of time's direction is elusive.

Coveney and Highfield in their work *The Arrow of Time* have addressed themselves to the problem of scientific proof of the direction of time.

They point out that science by and large has ignored the importance of time; that time has not been given, in scientific thinking, its prime place; and that even the laws of relativity would be applicable in the same way if time were reversed and the flow was from the future to the past.[2]

All the great achievements in the formulation of scientific laws and systems, be they by Newton, or Einstein, or Heisenberg and Schrödinger, work equally well with however time may flow, whether it has a forward movement or a reverse direction. The claim that time runs in one direction from the past to the future, may then appear as mental illusion, which some scientists – despite what common sense may tell us of the matter – dismiss contemptuously as 'psychological time' or 'subjective time'.

The authors then go on to posit the question as to whether there could be somewhere in the universe a direction of time contrary to the time we experience, a time which means that life goes from the grave and death, through a process of becoming younger and ends with birth – an existence where ripples converge in water and a stone is ejected from the point of that convergence.

The authors then go on to look at the macroscopic realm of cosmology expounding the question of that singularity of the beginning of the universe known as the 'Big Bang' and the consequent expansion; the microscopic realm of quantum theory dealing with the properties of matter on the most minute scales and all the questions raised by the observation of light and energy behaviour; thermodynamics with all the significance of the dissipation of energy and the phenomenon of entropy; and biological questions, not least of all as to why there would be diversity in evolution and new forms of life thrown up.

In the consideration of all these and in the complexes of their – in many cases still unresolved – relationship one with another and with all others, the weight of probability is that time has a definite direction, the 'arrow' of time flying towards the future and therefore creating a past.

It is not for theology to pass judgment on the ability of science, save to enter into conversation with it to mutual advantage in mutual concerns – and to remind its practitioners (and itself, which it has from time to time lamentably failed to do) that we are but dust. Indeed, for theology to sit in the chair of judgment about the value of the findings of another discipline in whose processes of reasoning it has no skill, is discourteous, irrational and totally (as the seventeenth century would say) 'inconvenient'. The reverse is true; a fact which Stephen Hawking, for all his great insight, should have taken to himself in his work *A Brief History of Time*. Indeed, in his 1989 *Halley Lecture* in Oxford, he puts forward a concept of 'imaginary time' which is based on a theory upon another theory and so on. This can only be placed beside his critical observations regarding the existence of God and what is the more insubstantially grounded, judged.

However, it can only be to theology's advantage to read how another discipline tackles the intriguing mystery of time, raises questions and provides observations which have to be acknowledged, addressed and followed by all. There is revealed a mutual goal, which will never be reached in this dimension of time according to theology, but for which we must strive so that it becomes clearer as we stretch out towards it. And there are revealed mutual concerns and questions, particularly concerning the nature of time at its beginning and as we experience it, the place of humanity in this time, and the relation of light to time, with the nature and quality of light having to be considered in order to clarify this issue.

That we exist in a movement of time, the direction of which means that we have a past, a 'present' and a future, seems to be an area of broad agreement.

Theology, for its part, might tend to look at the nature of this dimension of time in which we live, move and have our being, by way of its quality as past, present and future, rather than its mathematical measurement. But in so doing, it can only add to the significance of time's measurement, even if it is thought to be speaking of what has been referred to above as *subjective time*. In fact it does not regard time as merely subjective, but it does bracket together profoundly time and human existence and experience. It knows no *imaginary time*, but it does speak of the contingent relation of our time, created time, to the uncreated Time which is God.

The subjective relativity of time and the dangers of that for thinking about the nature of time, have been mentioned already.[3] But this does not mean that there is no place for a due subjectivism. Indeed, this is the very factor which may be necessary for a balanced view of the nature of time, provided it is placed within the context of what we may observe and comment on with regard to the objective revelation of God and the contingent relation of all things to uncreated Time and Light.

For a moment we must turn to the question of individuality and time.

There is a general limitation of humanity according to theology, namely that it was created in and for a relationship with God. God declares himself in Christ to be man's God. As this he is

God. He is not another sort of God. Man (I use the term generically) cannot live, move and have his being apart from this relationship, or in any other relationship, and still be truly man – the man of God's creative intent. This general limitation is exhibited in the estate and vocation of man vis-a-vis both God and the other orders of creation. According to the biblical narrative, he is created as the Prophet, Priest and King of creation. He is to go out and explore the rest of creation, see its constituent parts, name them and give voice to thanksgiving for them (for without his rational mind and mouth they would be otherwise dumb) before God. He is to tend and care for creation. And he is to have dominion over it, being responsible for the maintenance of good order as God's vice-regent.

The general limitation of humanity is, therefore, that it is answerable to God for the fulfilment of its estate and the exercise of its vocation as that is determined as genuine humanity, God's humanity, in and by the creative counsels and decree of God. Christ is that genuine man, himself alone God's man, in whom all humanity finds its contingent relation.

Within that general limitation there are particular limitations. These are as many as there are individuals who have been, are or may yet be. Within the general summons giving place and role, there is a particular summons to each individual regarding diversity within the body politic of humanity. Strictly speaking, there is no such thing as humanity as theory in general, but only the individual in the totality of every individual's circumstances and span of days.

Each individual is a microcosm. He or she is summoned in and by the Creator Word as a microcosm which in its particularity hears the general summons. He or she can only be the individual which God requires him or her to be within that Word of God to all mankind, which Word comes in a specific and particular command to that individual. This command comes not in any arbitrary, happen chance, take-it-or-leave-it way, nor by accidental chance (much less through subjective piety or religious experience so called), but by the deliberation, direction and sure aim by which the shaft is loosed from the bow and finds it mark.

Theology speaks of a God Who is immense in the majestic sweep of his all-inclusive loving-kindness and grace in calling all things into being, and intense in the minute individual application of that loving-kindness and grace. We are concerned here both with the immeasurable depths of cosmic infinities and with the intricate establishment of specific individuality. It is the latter which is our immediate concern in what follows.

The biblical witness contains that emphasis which speaks of this latter. The limitations of the individual are contrasted with the God who is beyond comparison to any created thing:[4]

> Then the Lord answered Job out of the whirlwind and said, 'Who is this that darkeneth counsel by words without knowledge? ... Where wast thou when I laid the foundations of the earth? declare if thou hast understanding. Who hath laid the measures thereof, if thou knowest? or who hath stretched the line upon it? Whereupon are the foundations thereof fastened? or who laid the cornerstone thereof; when the morning stars sang together, and all the sons of God shouted for joy? [the verse with Grosseteste interpreted as indicating the creation of angels] ... Where is the way where light dwelleth? and as for darkness, where is the place thereof, and that thou shouldest know the paths to the house thereof? Knowest thou it, because thou wast then born? or because the number of thy days is great?'

In this way part of biblical thought contrasts God and man by way of challenge to fathom the mysteries of the act of creation and reminder that man's days are his bonds, his fetters and his bounds. So we are therefore concerned immediately with the limitation of individual life – with the existence of any individual. This limitation is twofold, but there is an inextricable relation between, and an essential unity of, the two. It is the span of days which is that individual's existence and what that man or women peculiarly is within that measurement.

The apparent brevity of that span is a constant complain. That his days are *swifter than a weaver's shuttle,*[5] a withering flower of a day, a fleeting shadow,[6] a ship that passes, the swoop of an eagle,[7] as an handbreadth,[8] is man's repititious melancholy.

Within this short and fleeting span, too, man is likely to be discontent with what he is and what has befallen him. He habitually frets with envy at the supposed success of the unscrupulous.[9] He is inclined little enough to be content with what, according to the 'ungodly', is the poverty and littleness of the lot of the 'God-fearing'.[10] It is rare for him to be content in and with whatever state is his,[11] or to have appreciated the necessity of seeing his being grounded in his Creator by petitioning *make Thy way plain before my face*,[12] and thus to rest on the acknowledgement *my times are in Thy hand*.[13]

Restless dis-satisfaction tends to characterize the individual. But when the biblical reporting and exclaiming of such is examined, it may become apparent that at the root of such bewailing lies the failure to appreciate time in its context, and thus to look at time as a masterful fate which inevitably ravages us, and crumbles us into dust.

In other words, time is regarded as the force of entropy, and therefore as being a horizontal measurement only. Here such attitudes of mind emphasize the measurement of time, and fail to grasp that time is more than human calculation.

There is another biblical emphasis which is born of the Hebraic mind and its way of thinking. And this that time is not to be looked at in quantitive terms only but in qualitative. That is, what characterizes time is not its length or shortness, but what happens within it. But even that is not enough for a due regard of time. For not only is the complaining mind concerned with the measurement of time, and therefore time by itself as an independent thing, but it is also concerned with the apparent injustices that occur within time. That they are seen as such is countered by the Hebraic mind in its reminder that time is related to its source and qualified by the nature of that source.

Unless that is appreciated, any scrutiny of time for the individual can only be a haphazard and disordered jumble of succeeding shapes – rather as may be seen lying in a kaleidoscope. But when the kaleidoscope is shaken from inertia in the hand of the viewer and applied properly to the eye, then out of disorder is seen to come the most intriguing and intricate order of well patterned shapes. Even the crises which afflict the individual are made part of the order within the whole and of the whole.

There is, of course, a proper restlessness of spirit and complaining which is the desire to come to terms with the significance and establishment of these limitations, and view them in their context. It is a desire to find meaning with regard to time and what the individual is in his or her time. It is that struggle to apprehend the revelation of time's relativity and relation to that which has brought it into being.

It is this restlessness and its eventual rest of which Augustine speaks:[14]

> Thou has made us for Thyself and restless is our heart until it comes to rest in Thee.

Or that contentment expressed by St Paul, who had learnt to be so in whatever circumstance he found himself.[15]

This restlessness, endeavour and resolution is, as far as theology is concerned, the bringing of the individual into the right orientation with his or her Creator. The principle here is the recognition of contingency to and from God. This involves the coming to terms with the limitations given by the Creator and the appreciation of our creaturehood in relation to the Creator.

The entrance to this knowledge is the fact that the Creator himself is no stranger to these limitations and that state of being a creature. In Christ he has made them his own. He himself knows the metal of which we are made and the mould in which we are cast. So, when the word of God is addressed to the individual, he is nigh and speaks to his own. God in his Word knows man. For man is his creation, his handiwork and his possession, whom God will have – despite all that seems to mitigate against this – as his friend. The accolade accorded to Abraham and Moses[16] whereby they are called *friends* of God, is re-asserted universally for all by the Creator Word made flesh.[17] The Incarnation is the establishing of the bond of friendship, that is, the right contingent relation, between God and man, in which we, as 'personalised persons' are held in the grace and love of the Creator Word as the 'Personalising Person'.

This means that each can ponder on the fact that in his or her very limitations – the span of time which is ours, the endowments, vocations and enabling from God which makes the individual what he or she is in that measure of years – our significance and purpose is found within that contingent relation of friendship, which is the determination by God of these limitations. There is as great a diversity as there are individuals, but *it is the same God Who worketh all in all.*[18]

This leads to the conclusion that we have to rid ourselves of the idea that our limitations are a curse, a burden, something unjust and essentially degrading. Our limitations are none other than the affirmation by God as who and what each individual is. We are so defined by God. If we were not, we would be characterless, un-personal, shapeless and void.

When God addresses man through the Creator Word, and

calls him to this estate and realization, he does not deny our human nature and being with the command to become something other than we are. Rather, he establishes man as genuine man, that is, man as in His creative intent, God's humanity corresponding to what God wills us to be. This realization is evoked from the Psalmist [19] – not by way of arrogance, but in thankful awe – linking us in our respective times to that uncreated Time of God's creative act in the genre of Hebrew thought:

> I will praise Thee: for I am fearfully and wonderfully made; marvellous are Thy works, and that my soul knoweth right well. My substance was not hid from Thee, when I was wrought in secret, and curiously wrought in the lowest parts of the earth. Thine eyes did see my substance being yet unperfect; and in Thy book were all my members written, which in continuance were fashioned, when as yet there was none of them.

God differentiates the creature from himself and gives it its specific and genuine reality as his creature. But what the above thought forms, expressed in the Hebrew idiom, seem to point to, is the fact that that differentiation and establishment in the creation of the individual, takes place 'before' the individual is brought into being in his or her time. That is to say, we have the hint here that we are determined in the creative counsels and act of God at the instant of creation; that we are present in the will, decision and act of God in his Word by whom all things are made.

This is to claim that our existence and our time is present, and we already named, known and loved by God, in the beginning – that singularity whereby all creation is brought into being, and therefore wherein all creation is brought into being. It is therefore to claim that all existence and time is recapitulative in that singularity and that our respective existences and times – the existences and times of all individuals – are the horizontal refraction expressed in a dimension of passing from past through 'present' to future, of that recapitulative instant wherein all time is present to God.

But more than this, for this can imply that the One who is God's man, the very Image of God who is such because he images what he is, Christ himself, is present at that creative singularity. The flesh which the Word assumed, and the human existence of that Word in incarnation is 'simultaneous' with the creative utterance of the eternal Word, *Let there be: Let us make.*

What we are striving for here is the way of expressing Incarnation and Creation to be profoundly bracketed together as the mode of creation. We are also attempting to say that recapitulation in Christ, confined by Irenaeus to the significance of the Incarnation in time as the point in time where all time and all things are gathered up in their relation to the Word who created them and who is now flesh in time, is the self-same recapitulation in which all things are brought into being in the *beginning*.

This would add an even more profound dimension to St Paul's observation that we are already dead and risen in Christ, that our life is hid with God in Christ, in whom all fulness dwells.[20]

We are back at Grosseteste's question as to whether or not the Incarnation would have taken place had there not been a fall of man, and giving the unequivocal answer as 'Yes', for Incarnation is the context in which Creation is to be seen, and not Incarnation as a measure taken by God after Creation, having been accomplished, is seen to be in need of repair. We come back to the point that if the latter is the case, as is generally accepted by 'orthodox' thought, then God is contingent upon evil. We must ask the 'orthodox' to think again carefully on this matter.

If the former is the case, then we are faced with the possibility that if the process of creation, as we have already stressed, is not spread out in time, that is, that dimension of our time, but itself is accomplished in a twinkling in the creation of light, then all created time and existence is present for God at the 'point', that singularity of light, where creation is brought into being.

We may remind ourselves of Gregory of Nyssa's observation:[21]

> All, I say, with any insight, however moderate, into the nature of things, know that the world's Creator laid time and space as a background to what was to be; on this foundation He builds the universe. It is not possible that anything which has come or is now coming into being by way of creation, can be independent of space or time. But the existence which is all-sufficient, everlasting, world-enveloping, is not in space, nor in time: it is before these, and above these in an ineffable way; self-contained, knowable by faith alone; immeasurable by ages; without the accompaniment of time; seated and resting in itself, with no associations of past or future, there being nothing beside and beyond itself, whose passing can make something past and something future. Such accidents are confined to the creation, whose life is divided with time's divisions into memory and hope. But within that transcend-

ent and blessed Power all things are equally present as in an instant: past and future are within its all-encircling grasp and its comprehensive view.

We are also confronted with the conclusion that the act of Incarnation and all that that involved is the characteristic of the creative act of God. Gregory of Nyssa again would seem to be pointing in this direction in his description of Christ as the *Proptotype* of humanity's creation.[22]

He is discussing in this particular passage the distinction between male and female, and how this accords with the phrase the image of God.

> I presume that every one knows that this is a departure from the Prototype: for 'In Christ Jesus', as the Apostle says, 'there is neither male nor female'. Yet the phrase declares man thus divided.

He then goes on to point out that this can only mean, since God is all-good and only creates in goodness, that humanity, as male and female, are participants of the goodness of God which is *his image*. The conclusion would seem to be that the creation of humanity (and therefore all creation, as there can be no projection of temporal measurement into the creative act of God) is to do, certainly with the eternal Word by whom all things are made, but also with that Word made flesh, that is creation in the image of God which is Jesus Christ. Again Incarnation and Creation are inseparably bound together.

What we are trying to point to here is that God knows the cost of creating that which is other than himself, and therefore liable to imperfection, and that the decision to create involves, in his goodness, grace and love, the commitment of his being to that creation in Incarnation. Therefore in the uncreated Time of God, the *beginning* by which God is not only Father of the Son and Son of the Father in the bond of eternal Love, the Holy Spirit, but is Creator too, involves the time of Jesus Christ, incarnate, crucified, resurrected and ascended, as the foundation act of creation.

Perhaps the seventeenth century theologian John Swan's observations in his *Hexameron* concerning the nature of time in relation to 'eternity' are pertinent,[23] taking, in this context, a meaning which Swan did not see in their fulness.

Time, by whose revolutions we measure houres, dayes, weeks, moneths and years, is nothing else but (as it were) a certain space borrowed or set apart from eternitie; which shall at the last return to eternitie again: like the rivers, which have their first course from the seas; and by running on, there they arrive, and have their last: for before Time began, there was Eternitie, namely God; which was, which is, and which shall be forever: without beginning or end, and yet the beginning and end of all things. *Aeternitas enim, Dei Solummodo natura substantialiter inest*, saith one: that is, Eternitie is substantially onely in the nature of God.

All this raises questions of God's 'eternal' omnipotence and omniscience, and of possible consequent temporal determinism. It is to these that we now turn.

6
Predestination, Universalism and Time

THE CONSIDERATION of the omnipotence and the omniscience of God has led to what is wrongly called the doctrine of predestination. Predestination, as a theological statement does not reside there, as though these were attributes of God in isolation, but is, in its biblically based form, a Christological concern. It is unfortunate that in common thought the word *predestination* is immediately conceived as meaning that doctrine as stated by the Federal Calvinists, and is falsely attributed to John Calvin himself. There is a distinction of great magnitude between predestination as expounded by Calvin and the Geneva influenced reformers, and that put forward by the Federal Calvinists, centred on the Low Countries. From the latter, England learned her 'Calvinism' through the returned Marian exiles in the reign of Elizabeth, from the former, Scotland. This is best illustrated by the fact that there is a world of difference between the theology of the *Scots Confession* of 1560 and the work of the seventeenth century catechisms of the Westminster Divines.

There are two erroneous views of the doctrine of predestination. One is that of outright opposition to any such idea that the destiny of anyone – or anything – is predestined at all. This makes the objection that if the election of man for salvation is a matter of positive action on the part of God alone, then the rejection of man to damnation must be caused likewise. The second view would agree. This is the view historically of the Federal Calvinists who clung to a doctrine of double predestination – that God had, from all eternity, determined the number and identity of the elect, and, equally the number and identity of the rejected. This also further disintegrated into what was really a fatalism; that circumstances and events were caused by the will of God.

The first dismiss the doctrine of the second as a monstrous tenet, which it is; but not more so than the opinion of the first that man is the master of his own soul and captain of his salvation.

The doctrine of predestination properly outlined admits neither of synergism (man working his salvation with God by the exercise of his supposed free-will) nor of any projection of the cause of man's rejection into the active will of God. Nor does it tear Christ away from his proper context, the Divine life of the Trinity as the Word who was made flesh, making him, on the one hand, but an example or encouragement to the right exercise of man's freedom, or, on the other, but the means of establishing the decrees of God. He is, states the doctrine of predestination, the decree of God for all creation.

Underlying these views are, on the one hand, an elevation of the concept of man's free-will on the basis of an optimism concerning human nature, and on the other the positing of a decision made by God in all eternity behind the back of Christ as it were. The one assumes that there is such a thing as free-will, the other that it has plumbed the decrees of God to their depth. Of the latter, Lancelot Andrewes[1] in his sermon on the resurrection appearance of Christ to Mary Magdalen, *St John, chapter 20, verse 17 – Jesus saith unto her, Touch Me not* – wrote:

> ... (God's secret Decrees? May not they, for their height and depth, claim to this Noli (touch not), too?: Yes, sure: and I pray God Hee be well pleased with this licentious touching, nay, tossing His Decrees of late; this sounding the depths of His Judgements with our line and lead; too much presumed upon by some, in these days of ours ... (Saith the Psalmist) His judgements are the great deepe. St Paul, looking downe into it, ranne backe, and cried, O the depth! the profound depth! not to be searched, past our fadoming or finding out. Yet there are in the world that make but a shallow of this great deepe: they have sounded it to the bottome. God's Decrees, they have then at their fingers ends, can tell you the number and order of them just, with 1, 2, 3, 4, 5. Men that (sure) must have beene in God's Cabbinet, above the third heaven, where St Paul never came. Mary Magdalene's touch was nothing to these ...

It must be noted that the Laudian Divines of the seventeenth century, such as Andrewes, use the term 'Calvinist' in an ambivalent way – sometimes deploring it, sometimes applauding it. But this apparent contradiction is removed when the distinction between Calvinism proper and Federal Calvinism is appreciated. So Andrewes can criticize those who have God's decrees (that is double predestination) at their finger-tips, yet also write:[2]

> ... the best Writers both old and new (I name of the new, Mr
> Calvin; and of the old, St Augustine) ...

while Laud himself could instance Calvin's *Commentary on Psalm
118* in the introduction to his *Relation of the Conference*.[3]

The Christocentric emphasis of John Calvin on predestination
is of note in a consideration of the possible unitary relation between creation and incarnation with regard to the nature of time.

> As for the certain and distinctive foundation of the catholic faith,
> it is Christ.'For other foundation', said the Apostle, 'can no man
> lay save that which has been laid, which is Christ Jesus'.[4]

Calvin takes this point from Augustine and enlarges upon it,
emphasising the Christocentric nature of predestination. Christ is
the

> manner in which God discharges His work of grace ...,[5] bright
> mirror of the eternal and hidden election of God ...,[6] most
> excellent luminary of grace and predestination ...[7]

But the role of Christ in God's predestination is not only noetic.
It is also ontic. He is not only the revelation of God's creative
purpose for humanity, he is also in himself that which he reveals
– he is the content and substance of predestination, predestination
itself and the fulfilling of it. He is in himself God's decision
about man, and man's response to God, his 'amen' to God's
decree. Hence anything apart from Christ, any supposed decision
of God or any supposed freedom of man, is theologically invalid.

Citing Augustine's *De Praedestinatione Sanctorum VII*, Calvin
asserts that Christ is the *head*, that is the *fount*, the *sum*, the
recapitulation of predestination:[8]

> ... Let our head appear as the origin of grace, which flows
> through all members, according to the measure of each ... the
> One predestined to be our head, so many of us as are predestined
> to be His members.

Apart from Christ, election has no significance; predestination
is very much a matter of *in Christ*.

Calvin clearly states[9] that the decree of God and the title
given to Christ as *the Lamb slain from the foundation of the world*,
are one and the same thing.

> Peter ... puts high above all causes the decree which God
> determined in Himself. It is as if he had said they are now
> [that is, at the decree made by God] to reckon themselves
> among the sons of God, because before they were born they
> were elected. On this ground in the same chapter [Acts II] he
> teaches that Christ was foreordained before the foundation of
> the world to wash away the sins of the world by His sacrifice.
> Without a doubt, this means the the expiation of sin executed
> by Christ was ordained by the eternal decree (*scito*; *Beza has
> consilio*) of God. Nor can what is found in Peter's sermon
> recorded by Luke be otherwise and explained. Christ was deliv-
> ered to death by the determinative counsel and foreknowledge
> of God.

Here three factors are brought together – the *determinative*,
that is, implying the plan or design; the *counsel*; and the *foreknowledge*. These are held together and seen as a decision, a conversation, and a disposition within the Godhead – an activity of
Father, Son and Holy Spirit in concord. It is the failure to
appreciate the necessity of this necessary union of these three
aspects and to anchor them within the unity of Being of the
Trinity, which has led to the disparagement, and therefore the
dismissal of, the doctrine of predestination as a piece of fatalistic
thought expressed in causes and effects, means and ends – a
mechanistic determinism. Indeed it may be said that the Federal
Calvinists by their particular formulation of such predestinarianism, paved the way for the Deists and rationalists of the late
17th–18th centuries to rediscover the Prime Mover who had
constructed and set in motion a universe mechanically and irrevo-
cably determined.

But Calvin, in his Christocentric predestinarianism emphasises
the union of these three aspects:[10]

> Peter thus joins foreknowledge with counsel, that we may learn
> that Christ is not driven to death by chance or by the violent
> assault of men [the French edition adds, possibly by way of
> clarification 'as if He had been constrained to suffer their will'],
> but because God, the most good and the wise knower of all
> things, had deliberately so decreed it.

What is of import here is neither an historical resumé of
Calvin's doctrine of predestination, nor a discussion about how
he sees the apportionment of the so called elect and reprobate or
rejected worked out, but the strong emphasis found in his

statement of predestination that Christ stands central in the
eternal decree of God for humanity and creation.

We may suggest that the notion of predestination as stated by
Calvin is a theological endeavour to overcome a problem set up
by a view of time which could not be other than it was, given
the circumstances of the development of thought in which Calvin
was historically placed.

But out of the strictures of sixteenth century theological
thought, are there not pointers to the necessity of a bolder
affirmation that God, knowing the fragility of the result of creating
that which of necessity is lesser than he, having its own freedom,
dimension, nature and quality (its contingency from God) which it
can only maintain in its relation to, and dependency upon, him its
Creator (its contingency to God), makes provision for that?

In other words, the design, decree and act in creating is for
God the agonizing of love whereby his very Being is affected.
Creation can only mean Incarnation; *Let there be*, *Let us make*,
can only mean *the Word was made flesh*; the bringing of the
instant of light out of the darkness of nothingness can only mean
resurrection from the void of death.

The *new beginning* for God, whereby He 'is now' also Creator
and the One by whom all things are created, as well as Father
and Son, means that the Word 'is now' also incarnate and as such
crucified, dead, buried, risen and ascended. Could this not be the
beginning and the end, the first and the last, to which the
doctrine of predestination in its historical strictures was striving
to reach? Is not the identification of Incarnation and Creation in
that instant creative act of God the real content of predestination
– that God takes created time into the all-encircling embrace of
his uncreated Time?

T. F. Torrance,[11] following Athanasius, puts forward the
following statement:

> ... when the Scriptures tell us that 'in the beginning God
> created' we must understand 'beginning' in a twofold way: with
> reference to the creating act of God, and with reference to what
> He has created [ἔργα]. Hence Athanasius could say that 'while the
> works have a beginning in being made, their beginning precedes
> their coming to be'. Behind the beginning of creation there is an
> absolute or transcendent beginning by God who is himself
> eternally without beginning. This is what makes the creation of
> the world out of nothing so utterly baffling and astonishing. It is

not only that something absolutely new has begun to be, new even for God who created it by his Word and gave it a contingent reality and integrity outwith himself, but that in some incomprehensible way, to cite Athanasius again, 'the Word himself became the Maker of things that have a beginning' ... It is in similar terms that we may speak of the eternal Son who became man. The Son was always Son of God, but now He is Man as well as God.

A reading of this section leads to the conclusion that Professor Torrance is postulating two new beginnings for God. If this is the case, and the Incarnation is the second beginning, does this not reduce the Incarnation in the last resort to that which is merely economic? Far be it from me, with the Psalmist, to be more learned than my teachers, but I pose this question in all respect, for (and here I may not be wiser than my teachers) I cannot see how, if there is a necessity for yet another, second beginning for God, that this does not imply that God is contingent upon evil – that is, that he has not had the acumen to foresee the estate into which humanity has come, and therefore had to do something about it. I am sure that Professor Torrance would never hold to such a view as the contingency of God, but is it not unavoidable in this positing of a second beginning?

Of course, the argument could be made that the Incarnation was in the creative will of God, and only took the form it did, of suffering and death on the Cross, because of the 'Fall'. Had there been no 'Fall', it would have taken a happier form. But I must ask again, does this not mean that God is contingent on the circumstances of time, and on the freedom of his creatures? It seems to be that this dependence of God on his own handiwork can only be avoided by the fact that the 'two beginnings' are only seen as such in the dimension of time as we know it, but are one in the uncreated Time of God, in the instant where all time is present in the act of the God who in creating involves his whole Being as Father, Son and Holy Spirit, in design, plan and act, making Incarnation the basis of Creation, the *fundamentum* by which all things are brought out of nothing, and in which they live, move and have their being.

Then predestination consists of the fact that the Incarnation, as the new beginning of God, is that stone which is both the sure foundation and the stone of stumbling, for all creation. It is this because it is the way for creation and there is no other way, it being the decree, the design and the act of God. Only in this context can creation be that creation willed by God, and humanity be God's humanity. If humanity seeks another way, then Christ confronts it as a rectifying constant, which is the love of God's decree to uphold His handiwork faithfully, even in its faithlessness. In this way, the love of God is also the judgment of God.

If Christ is the predestination of God for all creation, he is also its recapitulation, and if its recapitulation then its predestination. For, according to the Epistle to the Colossians [12]

> He is before all things, and in Him all things hold together . . . For God willed all fulness [πλήρωμα – creation's totality] to dwell in Him, and through Him to reconcile all things, whether on earth or in heaven, making peace by the blood of His cross.

He is the *head* summing up all creation. But he is that at the 'point' where creation and incarnation are one in the uncreated Time of God, the beginning 'preceding', in the Triune existence, the coming into being of all things, and, as such, the One by whom they are brought into being. Recapitulation, as understood by Irenaeus, namely the summing up of all things in Christ in time, is only one side of the coin. The other is that this is the expression in time of that which is within the uncreated Time of God. It is tempting to say that Irenaeus's doctrine of recapitulation tended to fade in theological thought in the centuries subsequent, for it was not fully grounded being inadequately related to the creative act of God in his Word and the relation therefore of created time to uncreated Time.

Here again we may apply the illustration of the single beam of light (all things and all time in that creative singularity which is the new beginning for God in his uncreated Time) refracted into what we experience as centuries, decades, years, months, days, hours. This three-dimensional existence of ours, is all contained in that singularity for God, wherein all creation and all time in the freedom of its created contingency from God, is ordered and held together, past and future in a fulfilled present.

If this radical view of the existence of all things recapitulate in that beginning, is taken, then predestination is none other than the name of Jesus Christ. But, if this is the case, recapitulation, predestination and universalism are seen to be one and the same thing, or, at least, different aspects of the one Name.

But before looking at the meaning of universalism in this light, the question of what evil is, has to be considered.

Straight away a warning can be issued about the subject of evil. That there should be that which is opposed to light, life, order, and harmony in created life, is irrational. That is the point about evil – that it is irrational, and cannot be made to fit into any rational explanation. Indeed the very way in which evil seems to operate is by being found intriguing and being given place therefore. That which is irrational cannot be explained rationally. We may waste little time on it, save to note that it is a serious business. To spend time on it and become engrossed with it, may result, as Karl Barth warned, on us becoming a little demonic ourselves.

What little we may say is that it seems to operate by seeking to shatter the delicate balance of contingency – to interrupt the relation between contingency to God (creation's dependence on him) and contingency from God (creation's identity, quality and nature within its own dimension). It seems to exaggerate the contingency from at the expense of the contingency to.

This lies behind the understanding of the biblical narrative of the Fall. The temptation to the man is to ignore what God has decreed as that which is good, that is, the order which he has bestowed in creating all things (and by implication his 'No' to any other ordering). The temptation to humanity is to construct standards of good and evil for itself, and be the judge of them. Humanity is enticed to forgo any thought of dependency upon God and therefore to deny its purpose and nature of origin and to become as a god, ordering all things in freedom from God. Humanity is therefore tempted to elevate the sense of contingency from God, and to declare itself free.

The example of the cancerous cell may be apt here. Here is the attempt by a cell to free itself from its proper context in which alone it can be what it is meant to be and function correctly. It assumes an existence and a direction of its own, with lamentable consequence.

The fragility of creation is its delicate balance between contingency to and contingency from God. But if it is to be a creation which is free within its creative given-ness by God, then this balance has to be. Otherwise it is but a deterministic phenomenon, a mechanism without the quality to be itself in that freedom towards its Creator, which this double contingency alone can give.

That God knows that what is created will possess this fragility is why the Word, by whom all things are created, takes flesh and nature to himself – but at that point where, in the embrace of uncreated Time, created time is brought into being, and is recapitulate in all its span at its inception by that Word. All time is under the compulsion of its contingency through and in and by the Word made flesh. The act of creation by the Word is also the act of taking its fragility, the consequences of its free contingency, upon himself and to himself.

In this way, it is suggested, creation and incarnation are radically bracketed together.

In a strange sense, God is the cause of evil. By the very act of creating an entity other than himself, that is with a contingency from him in order to give it its own life and nature, he opens the possibility of its self-assertion over against himself. But this is contained in the contingency to him, its dependence on him for its life and nature. Its freedom can only be freedom in this context. In other words true created freedom is freedom towards and for God, otherwise it is self-destructive freedom. This tension and crisis, this contradiction between contingency to and contingency from, is resolved in the Word made flesh, where the double contingency is in equilibrium and harmony, where the existence of the man Jesus is creation's perfect response to the will and decree and act of God, its 'Amen' to his creative intent.

The crisis of creation is the will of God that the Word bears this contradiction and resolves it. While we may say that creation is a matter of the love and grace of God, this crisis should not be ignored as it is the cost of creation to the very Being of God, and heightens the staggering value of that love and grace, which otherwise become a mere bland assertion of principle.

Augustine in beginning, and Calvin in clarifying, the principles of predestination, were quite correct when viewed in this context. The primary cause of 'salvation' is the will of God; the secondary cause is the response of man evoked by the sense of the grace and love of God. The primary cause of 'rejection' is the will of men in rejecting that grace and love; the secondary cause is the very presence and fact of that love and grace which is rejected.

But are we right in thinking in terms of 'rejection'? Certainly dreadful things are caused by the imbalance of double contingency, where humanity in its will and creation in its direction are seen to go their own way with dire results. Can 'rejection' be a factor in God's creative will? The double predestinarians would answer in the affirmative. Even those who abhor and deny such a doctrine and who take a stand on the free-will of man have the same dilemma. For if by the exercise of free-will 'rejection' results, then the same conclusion is reached that God 'rejects' even if that 'rejection' does not reside in, and is caused by, his foreordained decree.

To say that God does not reject offends our innate sense of justice. A universalism which implies a morally disinterested God surely cannot be countenanced. How can wrong and evil be ignored by a God of righteousness?

It is here that the marriage of predestination proper and universalism provide an answer to the problem of God creating in love and grace and goodness and yet having to deal with evil and wrong. Indeed universalism need not imply a morally disinterested God, and this sort of universalism is the corollary to a Christocentric predestinarianism.

The statements on *Universal Salvation* and *Judgement* by Jacques Ellul[13] have much to offer here if they are placed within the context of the simultaneity of incarnation and creation as the new beginning in the uncreated Time of God.

Ellul begins with what may be seen as a basic contradiction *ad absurdum* concerning the concept of hell. His introductory thesis is that if God is almighty, omnipresent, the Creator of all, then there can be no place or being outside him, otherwise he would not be what he is claimed to be. Nor is there any place where he, if he be omnipresent, is not present. Hell is therefore either part of God, or a place where he is not. Both are absurd.

In the midst of a rather questionable argument concerning the concept of *creatio ex nihilo*, creation out of nothing, he makes the very valid point that for creation to revert to nothingness would imply a negation of God. God withstands nothingness and constantly upholds creation against its ever-present threat, for creation is the object of his love. This fact that God is love is revealed in Christ, the central revelation. For God to cease loving would be a contradiction in terms.

The outcome of all this is that nothing can exist outside God's love, for God is all in all. It is unthinkable, argues Ellul, that there could be a hell, a place of suffering under the domination of evil.

If we take the thesis that God creates all things by his Word in love, and in love makes provision for the fragility of creation by that Word incarnate as the way of creating, then, to heighten Ellul's argument, it is utterly impossible for there to be a hell such as has been conceived in historical theology. His Word contains all things in his embrace of love from the *beginning*. That is the will, decree and act of God at the *beginning* within his uncreated Time. From the beginning then, and in the creative decree of God, hell is excluded as a possibility. Indeed hell can only be a concept thrown up in order to explain that there is justice for all that is against God when time is regarded as a thing in itself and by itself. It is an attempt to seek compensating justice in a supposed world to come, because the idea of time in this world is an inadequate framework within which to perceive the height and depth of such issues related to the uncreated Time of God's existence.

So much of the theological endeavour is undertaken within the constrictions of mere three-dimensional thought – attempts to deal with the problems raised by time without taking the nature of time in relation to God as uncreated Time, into consideration. Such theological activity is then literally a waste of time and is as absurd as its context – double predestination, hell and blind universalism being two such instances of such three-dimensional absurdities of thought.

Ellul's universalism is not blind, for it is regarded in the light of the Word made flesh, even if, like Calvin and his doctrine of predestination, it is not related to the uncreated Time of God and the beginning for God within that, and incarnation and creation brought together radically. In this respect he underlines the claim[14] that God has directed his own justice upon himself in Christ, the condemnation of our wickedness.

Ellul takes the issue of the judgment passed on Christ, first, and asks why, if this judgment were sufficient, there should be a further judgment on individuals. Was the price Christ, the Son of God, paid insufficient? Did it not meet the measure of the demands of God's justice? His second point is that doubtless this justice has indeed been satisfied in God and by God for us, and that here we see and know only the love of God. This love manifests itself in all this as predestination But this predestination, which is God's love for us in Christ, therefore can only be a predestination in Christ and through Christ to salvation. In him, all people are predestined to be saved. Ellul's third development of this argument is that what is called 'free choice' is meaningless in this regard. It is foolish to think that God presents us with the Gospel of Christ in a take it or leave manner, deputing the final issue to be decided to us – namely whether we accept it and are saved or reject it and are damned. This leaves the whole issue upon our shoulders and as our total responsibility. Our decision is the authority in the matter, which, as he concludes, reverses a well-known thesis, so that now this elevation of our capacity in the matter means that God proposes and man disposes.

So Ellul argues. But if this act of love of God in Jesus Christ towards creation is applied to God's decree and act of creation, it is then seen not to be an addition to and a later repair of his handiwork (even if it is said that this was in his mind at creation), but the mode and cost of creation itself. God himself in his Word takes it and bears it that creation might be upheld even in its fragility. 'Salvation' then becomes our created destiny, a destiny not only for humanity, but for all creation with humanity at its heart. So the Epistle to the Romans[15] can speak of the waiting of creation groaning and travailing for its redemption and the liberty of the children of God. The *sufferings of this present time*, by which phrase St Paul introduces these observations, are in the context of suffering with Christ and being glorified with him. Here again, if these marks of the present creation's state are regarded as recapitulative in what God has undertaken in his Word at that *beginning* in uncreated Time, then the whole burden of this passage can be seen as the temporal working out of that which is already fulfilled as the destiny of all creation in the will, decree, act and involvement of God at creation, and not just in the temporal life of the Word made flesh as an adjunct to creation.

Universalism properly grounded in Christ as the decree and involvement of God in creating, regards nothing in creation as excluded or lost. Rather, being recapitulative in Christ as the *Beginning*, the *Alpha*, everything is seen in that context as being declared by the Creator to be indeed *good*.

The *behold it was very good* of the Genesis narrative can only have validity if it is grounded on an already finished *beginning*, namely, incarnation and creation as two sides of the one 'event', where Christ is not only the *Beginning*, the *Alpha* but the *Omega*, the *End*, as well. On this the goodness, which is the essential, divinely ordained and achieved, origin of all creation and humanity, is grounded – otherwise the *behold it was very good* is hollow and tragic.

We need to excise the phrase *original sin* in theological vocabulary and moral consideration. This is not to dilute the strength of the ravages of evil, or to dismiss the terribleness of suffering. On the contrary, it lets them be seen to be the profound darkness which they are – but as that which God has already acknowledged, embraced and contained in his *new beginning* in and by his Word. Is this not that *crisis* to which Barth pointed in his earlier years, but a greater crisis than he then indicated? For it is the crisis in which we work out in time what is 'already' dealt with in that beginning. It is the crisis of the ultimate dialectic between created time and that *Beginning* in uncreated Time, the agony and the achievement of the love of the Creator. It is the crisis of the Beginning who is also the End, the singularity of God's creative act, worked out in our refracted time measured in divisions of past, present and future.

Ellul goes on to examine the biblical statements about judgment, condemnation and rejection, and finds that most interpreters and commentators do not look at these in context. He is convinced that the parables of Christ which deal with such themes are to encourage people to think what creation would be like without love, so that they may consider their life, its nature and its true destiny in the creative intent of God. They are not told to make people afraid, or to elevate hell and evil as articles of belief. Such a loveless creation would be hell, and that we can already experience in this time of ours.

His main point in his interpretation of the biblical texts, is that what is judged, condemned and rejected, is not beings but their works. Ellul finds that most of the texts speak of the consuming of evil works. However, so intimately connected are being and works that judgment will, of course affect being – but not to its annihilation in some hell. The greater the works of evil, the more diminished the person in the refining fire of God's judging love. But being is still the creation of God which he will not lose.

His insistence on the sufficiency of Christ's sufferings to the discarding of any idea that there must still be a place of eternal suffering, as the traditional view has it, is the hallmark of a proper universalism which does not evade the demands of a righteous God, the disaster of contradicting the intent of our creation, and which is in simple harmony with the predestination of God for all creation which lives, moves and has its being in its time in that fulfilled Present in the uncreated Time of God, His Word made flesh, the Creator taking creation into union with himself at its beginning, the Beginning which is also the End.

It is a question of recognizing that God has reckoned with creation in that Beginning in which he is also Creator as well as Father and Son, rather than us, in our constricted vision in refracted time, reckoning with God and reducing him and his working to facile and eventually contradictory doctrines.

7

Time Created and Uncreated Time

KARL BARTH makes – at least to minds which seek to pursue in a three-dimensional mode theological questions and answers concerning God and man, Creator and creation, in the context of what they construe to be the nature of time and eternity – an astonishing and even an incomprehensible statement.[1] At a cursory reading he might be thought at first to be advocating that eternity is endless time:

> Even the eternal God does not live without time. He is supremely temporal. For His eternity is authentic temporality, and therefore the source of all time.

That superficial interpretation is dispelled by what Barth wishes to convey by his use of *authentic time*. By that use he also cuts across any supposed theological attitudes based on prior conceptions about time. Our time is to be interpreted in terms of what he means by this *authentic time* of the Creator, rather than the way in which God exists being construed in terms of some understanding about time which we assume as self-evident from our existence. Indeed in the light of God's *authentic time*, our understanding of our time and existence takes on a new perspective as well.

There is no such thing as 'eternity' which God happens to inhabit, and in so inhabiting this dimension is thereby God. Eternity does not make God God. Rather, because God is the God he is, there is what we call 'eternity'. This is the same observation already noted as made by John Swan:[2]

> *Aeteritas enim, Dei Solummodo natura substantialiter inest*, saith one: that is, Eternitie is substantially only in the nature of God.

God is what is called 'eternity': what is called 'eternity' is God. Barth describes this 'eternity' as *authentic temporality*. By this he means

> ... in the uncreated self-subsistent time which is one of the perfections of His divine nature, present, past and future, yesterday, today and tomorrow, are not successive, but simultaneous.

In the same way, we do not speak of created time as a reality in and for itself. It too, is self-subsistent, a secondary product of creating but, for all that, an unavoidable and inevitable one. It is a *form* of created existence. So Barth:[3]

> We speak of 'created time', but it would be more accurate to say 'co-created'. For time is not a something, a creature with other creatures, but a form of all the reality distinct from God, posited with it, and therefore a real form of its being and nature.

This being the case the use by Barth, or at least his translators, of the word *inauthentic* to describe created time, is perplexing. The word Barth uses in German is *uneigentlich*. *Authentic* (*eigentlich*) *temporality* for Barth is the simultaneity of God's Time. Eternity is not endless time, but that incomprehensible and inconceivable uncreated existence of God whereby God, because he is God, is the existence of uncreated simultaneity. If this is *authentic temporality* then this must mean that all temporality has its meaning here.

Barth's next stage of exposition is curious, for he goes on to speak of *man in his time*, but it is abundantly clear that he is not speaking of that category of time which he had previously regarded as the second of three[4] – the time created by God, our time (that is fallen time) and the time which God has for us in Christ.

It would appear that Barth has blurred his former categories, for here he speaks promiscuously of created time and man's temporality. We have to ask – if there is a distinction between time as created by God, and time which is ours (that is, 'fallen time') – what exactly Barth is meaning here, particularly as he goes on to speak of the Word taking this created time (and therefore surely fallen time) to himself in his uncreated Time at the incarnation. We can only say that he does not mention the distinction here. It would appear that in this context he is speaking of *man in his time* as the time given to creation by God which unfolds itself as a past, present and future, that dimension in which created beings can be what they are, that is with their identity, nature and quality which God intended for them.

The translators' use of the word which Barth uses to describe this time is *inauthentic*. This is perplexing. Do they mean *unauthentic*? Strictly speaking there is no such word as *inauthentic*.

The use of the word is certainly meant by Barth to distinguish the uncreated Time of God and created time. Professor T. F. Torrance, as an editor of *Church Dogmatics*, in conversation with me about this point, agrees that Barth does not disparage created time, and that the use of the word *inauthentic* as opposed to the strict translation *unauthentic* is meant to convey more significance than the stark negative.

He further agrees that contingency is implied here strongly and that the sense which *eigentlich* and *uneigentlich* conveys is, for the former *that which exists on its own right*, that is as God's uncreated Time, and for the latter, *that which does not exist on its own* but is dependent on the former for the distinctive nature which it has been given as created time.

It is Barth's wont to use individual words – and sometimes colloquially – as concentrated significances which are only unfolded within their context. Scrupulous care is required!

Double contingency, then, underlines Barth's understanding of time in this section of his *Church Dogmatics*.

This relation is revealed in God's self-revelation, the person and event of the Word made flesh. Here we have uncreated Time, that is, the Time of the Word as God, one with the Father and the Holy Spirit, taking to himself created time and living a human life and therefore living in this temporal dimension in relation to his fellow men. But this temporality of his in the flesh is lived out in his unity with God. This temporality, the span of his human life, is not only the exclusive time of one individual, but because he is this Individual, it is time for God and therefore for all humanity as his creation. In his temporal life, time becomes time for God and for all humanity. He ministers the things of God to man and the things of man to God, as Athanasius noted – he is the grace of God towards creation, and he is creation's response of gratitude and obedience towards God.

He exists as the man Jesus, with his own identity, but he does so in utter obedience to, and harmony with, God. The perfect, balanced and harmonious contingency presented in the human life of the Word is the principle of recapitulation. Although again Barth does not mention recapitulation explicitly in this section of

Church Dogmatics, it is clear that this is the logical inference which may be drawn from his argument.

What this means for time itself is suggested by that history of Jesus Christ after his death. This history, while it is still historical and observable, according to the biblical writers, is presented by them as more than three-dimension temporality. It is the history of the resurrection appearances and of the ascension.

It is a unique history, concerning this Individual alone. And yet all are affected by this history in their respective histories as individuals. It is in this resurrection history that the essential and indispensable key is placed to unlock what created time is in the embrace of uncreated time. This has nothing whatsoever to do with 'timeless' or 'spiritual' truths. It is the opening out of that embracing and embraced relation of the created and the uncreated within the observable realities of this time of ours. The true contingency of time is perceivable within time in this resurrection time of this Individual.

The burden of the witnesses and writers of the early Church is that the resurrection history of this man Jesus is precisely of the man Jesus, but of the man Jesus in the mode of God. In terms of time, this means that the resurrection reveals time as created time, but created time in its fulfilment in relation to uncreated Time. Just as this man Jesus had his time from birth to death, his own span of passing moments, his past, his 'present' and his future, and all this span came to an end, so his time is now not ended but fulfilled and thereby takes on a new dimension.

All that he had been and did, in temporal terms, is now gathered up into a dynamic and living present. This is the significance of his showing his wounds of crucifixion to the disciples – *behold My hands and side*. It is the same Jesus of Bethlehem, Nazareth, Gethsemane, Gabbatha and Golgotha, who so manifests himself to them now.

This may also be the significance of the grave clothes rolled up in a place by themselves, a lesser sign in the midst of the greater sign of the resurrection which is the empty tomb. Is this not a fitting symbolism of time in its refracted form, its direction and movement from the past to the future rolled up and discarded in that form, by the resurrection? Is it not a sign that that form of time (not time itself, but that form of it) which is characterised by entropy of life finding its equilibrium in death, is negated by the Creator's assuming of it and transforming it into resurrection?

In other words, time is declared to be more than it appears in our estimation and measurement of it into past, present and future. And it is other than it appears because of its contingent relation to the uncreated Time of God, which relation is actualised in the Word made flesh, declared in his resurrection, and sealed in his ascension.

The phrase πλήρωμα τόυ χρόνου, *fulness of time*, used by St Paul in Galatians, chapter 4, is significant for all this but often misinterpreted. It is sometimes thought that it means an evolution of time which has its climax in *fulness*. At that point God deemed it possible for the Word to be made flesh. Here is the idea that God fits his acts into a framework which is established independently of him – he fits himself into the movement of time as he sees time favourable to act. But this is hardly the case as it makes God dependent on created time, contingent to it. Certainly the Word came and entered created time and took it to himself. But it is because he came that the *fulness of time* comes. He brings the fulness with him; he does not come because the time was right and ripe. His advent as the Word made flesh and all that he is and accomplishes in the flesh in the dimension of created time, is the central point of all time. From the calculation of created time as past and future, time BC moved towards this point and moves on AD from it.

This does not mean that this particular time of this Man, with his history from birth to death and into resurrection history and ascension, is itself and merely itself, *fulfilled time*. It does not mean that the particular history of this Man is the πλήρωμα τόυ χρόνου, *fulness of all time*. The direction of time is not to and from the void, a meaningless movement without beginning and end. Its nature and direction is epitomized by this *fulness*. That is to say, time is determined by its fulfilled contingent relation with uncreated Time.

St Paul too implies a *Beginning* for God 'before' the *beginning* of creation. Here again I wish to depart from accepted views on the matter. To say, as traditional theology does, that God's decree in eternity is for his Son to be born, for the Word to be made flesh, at a given time, seems to suggest vaguely (no doubt not meaning consciously to do so) that God is contingent upon created time. This can, and has been, avoided by the claim that God's providence makes the time right – the choice of Israel to prepare for this, the rise of the Roman Empire to provide

propitious circumstances for the spread of Christianity, etc. All
this may be so. But I would suggest that in making this the
primary framework for God's providence it reduces theology
again to an argument of three-dimensional absurdity. What I am
asking is: does God's 'providence' stretch out only in our measurement of time and space?

I would agree here with some of the sentiments expressed by
David Jenkins, formerly Bishop of Durham, on such matters.
Equally, I am reminded of that illustration of facile ideas about
God's 'providence' by that aged and cantankerous character who
appears in cameo in one of Dorothy Sayers' novels,[5] who
complains bitterly if remarkably about Providence of whom she
has had enough, losing both her husband and her potatoes to his
decree, and observing that if Providence is not careful of his
ways, One above will deal with him.

The concept of providence, so often thoughtlessly used, is
shown in its absurdity when it is regarded as the way in which
God's decrees are worked out for and in our existence in time as
though it were the hand of God intervening when occasion
demands and bypassing all that has been once and for all
completed in and by Christ. It suggest a dualism, a gulf, between
uncreated Time and time created, which is bridged by the
reaching out and intervening finger of a remote and distant God,
this action being expressed by way of explanation in an artificial
framework labelled *providence*.

The same concept, albeit in a more erudite way, lurks behind
the Newtonian system of mathematics with its idea of dualism
between absolute time and space and relative time and space, for
this, in turn rests on a God who, for all practical purposes, is a
prisoner of his own absolute 'eternity' and whose mere interven-
tion is claimed only when happenings within created nature
require more than the ability of man can perceive.

Any union between time created and uncreated time would be
opposed to a Newtonian or any other dualism in the matter
wherein God is regarded essentially as a prisoner of his own
eternity able only to work that which is supernatural and inter-
vene in created time from a distance.

In seeking to further this unitary way of thinking regarding
the relation between created time and God's uncreated Time, I
would wish to plea for consideration of the idea that the *becoming*
of the Word – *The Word became flesh and dwelt among us, and we*

beheld his glory, the glory of the only-begotten of the Father, full of grace and truth – is, in the uncreated Time of God, the same as and one with the *becoming* of the Word – the Word *became* the *One by whom all things were made*, where previously the Father was only Father and the Son only the Son, but in this *beginning* become also the Creator and the One by whom all things are created. There is but one ἀρχή for God, one new beginning, where creation and incarnation are one, the latter being the mode of the former. A redemptionist theology and a creationist theology must be one. And if they are then the suggestion of the simultaneity of all created time within the uncreated present of God in the *Beginning* has much bearing on what the phrase *the fulness of time* means.

I find in Karl Barth's treatment of the phrase[6] much which calls out for an even more radical – that is, penetrating to the root – interpretation. He emphasises that his often repeated πλήρωμα τοῦ χρόνου. in the New Testament (referring first to Galations 4:1f) is not to be interpreted as meaning 'when the time was ripe' then God sent his Son into the world. That would be to imply that the historical situation and conditions reached a point where they were favourable for God to act, thus permitting him to do so, as though they had not been before, thereby inhibiting him. The act of God, Barth stresses, in sending his Son, in the Word becoming flesh, brings the *fulness of time* with it.[7]

> With the mission of the Son, with His entry into the time process, a new era of time has dawned, so far-reaching in its consequences that it may be justly called the fulness of all time.

But, as Barth goes on to say, this event does not make this particular time, that is, the time of the Word made flesh, the earthly days of Jesus of Nazareth from birth to death, fulfilled time. Fulfilled time.

> is before or after all other time.

Hence it makes all time fulfilled time.

> Time may seem to move into the void but it is actually moving towards this event, just as it may seem to move out of the void, but it is actually moving from this event. This fulfilment of time has now 'come', epitomising all the coming and going of time. Henceforth all time can only be regarded as time fulfilled in this particular time.

It seems to me that this, of itself, calls out for the perception that all time is relative to this *fulness of time* but that this *fulness* must reside in that singularity of the beginning of all creation and therefore of all time, which in turn is simultaneous with that New Beginning in God whereby he 'becomes' Creator. The point of relativity is the ἀρχή of time within the Ἀρχή in God's uncreated Time, which is the simultaneity of his becoming that which he was not 'before', namely Creator, with the becoming of the Word as flesh in the dynamic Present of God's Being.

This seems further called for as Barth goes on to relate two other New Testament themes as parallel with the *fulness of time*. The first of these is *recapitulation* (which again he seems not to emphasise sufficiently and give it its determinative place). The second is the *immanence of the Kingdom of God in the presence of Jesus Christ*.

The first is found in conjunction with the *fulness of time* in Ephesians, chapter 1, and here both these are pushed back into the decree and εὐδοκία, good pleasure of God *before the foundation of the world*.

> The One who wills and accomplishes and reveals the ἀνακεφα-λαίωσις (the gathering up in a head, the recapitulation) also wills and accomplishes and reveals the 'fulfilment of the times'. It is with the summing up of all created being in Christ as its Head that the καιροί – the individual times of individual created things – are not cancelled or destroyed but fulfilled. None of these times moved into the void. They all moved towards this goal, this event, and therefore this particular time.

Barth rightly goes on to say that the concept of *the time is fulfilled* in Mark, chapter 1, in conjunction with the drawing nigh of the kingdom of Heaven, has to be regarded as an emphatic and not a restrained statement, otherwise the whole passage is flat and banal, indicating merely a new era in the span of the ages.

But how, in the light of what Barth has just been writing about fulfilled time and its determinative relation to all time, can it be at that point in the minstry of Jesus, before passion, crucifixion and resurrection, fulfilled, unless, in terms of our measurement of time it is 'already' just that? This question is further deepened when he goes on to write[8] that the drawing nigh of the kingdom of Heaven in the coming of Jesus into Galilee preaching the gospel of God, means that this 'coming' is an irruption rather than mere immanence.

Yet Barth seems himself to flatten all this. He continues that this 'coming' is the fulfilment of the times, the gathering up of all things, concretely expressed in the drawing nigh of the kingdom in the coming of Jesus into Galilee at the beginning of his ministry. All this seems to beg to be taken further, for it still leaves, in Barth's account, the question of the relativity of time itself, all time, to this particular time of this particular coming. It may be said that it is so related because of the nature of the One who comes, the Creator of all. But this presupposes that he, being the One by whom all things were created, 'already' bears a relation to time. Is it then an incomplete relation which needs this further 'coming'? This must cast doubts as to the competence of God, the adequacy of what is called his 'foreknowledge' and his grip on his whole creation as a creation of time.

But if this 'coming' is an expression in our refracted time and its created realities of what is already fulfilled in the decree, act and accomplishment of God in creating – the decree, act and accomplishment whereby in his 'becoming' Creator he grasps all time in an instant to himself and deals with its created frailty so that in that Dynamic Present which is God's Uncreated Time, creation and incarnation are simultaneous – then there is indeed the actuality of the fulfilment of all time in this 'coming'.

Barth seems to lay down a disjunction between God and time when he continues that[9]

> In Him, the Son and heir of all things, in the kingdom of God which came to Galilee and was proclaimed in Galilee, all time is brought to an end and begins afresh as full and proper time.

But if, in Irenean terms, the end has not 'already' been joined to the beginning, what is this lacking and improper time? It can only be that which is adrift from God. If, on the other hand, the end has 'already' been joined to the beginning in the Beginning for God as Creator, then such statements can only be regarded as mythological explanations, in the terms of the language of our refracted time, of the freedom granted by God to his creation in its contingency from him yet nevertheless contained by him in its contingency to him. They can only be regarded, therefore, as mythological explanations, in the terms of the language of our refracted time, of what God 'foresees' and acts upon in the simultaneity in his Time of creation and incarnation. For what he surely 'foresees' is the consequence of creating at all, namely, the fact that creation and therefore time, because they are less than his own Perfections, will inevitably tend towards contingency from him at the expense of contingency to him if they are to have the freedom of their own dimension and nature and identity.

In the above quotation it is the phrase *begins afresh* which is unfortunate. For it does suggest that time went on, albeit moving towards this particular time of Jesus of Nazareth, yet only partially related to God who had not yet acted. It suggests that 'before the foundation of the world' what happened was a decree and a plan held in abeyance. It suggests that the suspension of that decree means that our temporality is projected into the Being of God. It suggests that time is a straight line, certainly with a beginning and an end, but nevertheless along which God moves being constrained by it. It seems to contradict Barth's own insistence that Christ brings the fulness of time with him.

We must reiterate: how can Christ bring the fulness of time with him if it is not 'already' present with him 'before' he came if it is not 'already' a reality in the Present of God's Being? How can he bring the recapitulation of all things, and therefore of time, with him, if that recapitulation was not 'already' present in the same way? And likewise, how can the kingdom of God draw nigh if it is not already in substance 'before' he came?

It is not enough to say that it is all present in the eternal decree of God, otherwise time intervenes between the decree and the fulfilling of it, and the process within the Divine existence thereby depends on time as we know it in its past, present and future. Is not this a subtle, even if unconscious, transference of temporal values and measurement into the Being and acting of God? And is there not lurking here a hidden subordinationism of the Word to the Father as the Father's agent who copes with wayward time in its three-dimensional aspect on behalf of the Father?

In passing it may be noted that this hint of subordination may skulk, again no doubt unintentionally, in Barth's observations in general on revelation and reconciliation, in his *Church Dogmatics*, vols. I:2 and IV:1 particularly.

But if the creative Act of God, the Beginning in the Being of God and the beginning of creation embraces in a twinkling all things and all time as a singularity *to God*; if God knows exactly what to create will involve and acts upon it in his decree and accomplishment of it, taking flesh and crucifixion to himself in order to allow creation its freedom and yet sustain it in relation to him; then the fulness of time, the recapitulation of all things, the kingdom of God is actual and present in all their reality in the 'coming' of Jesus of Nazareth. The phrase *the Lamb slain from the foundation of the world* is a matter of fact and accomplishment, not a matter of decree alone.

The time of Jesus of Nazareth, the recapitulation of all times and things, irrupting into our refracted times with their past, present and future at a given time (the years AD 1–33 for the sake of argument) is that time of God's new Beginning in himself simultaneous with that singularity which is the beginning of creation. To us it appears as part of our refracted time, as do all other events, and indeed it and they are so part. But its uniqueness consists in the fact that it is that part of the time of creation which reveals in substance all time as already present to God, begun and fulfilled instantly, in a twinkling, in his new Beginning and his creative act.

We are putting forward the possible concept that there are not two Beginnings for God separated by time – creation and incarnation – but only one. For God time is a dynamic Present wherein all time is gathered and contained, and from which the refraction of time so gathered and contained 'already' in God's uncreated Time is spread out in its nature in the created dimension which we know as past, present and future. The emphasis, we are saying, is not just on God in time in his Being and Person in the Word, but time in God's Being and Person in his Word by whom all things are made. Indeed, it is more correct to say that God in his Word comes *as* time, fulfilled time, and time exists with God in his Word as fulfilled time.

Perhaps we may expand this in the following way. The new Beginning for God means that in his uncreated Time all time and things are created in their double contingency instantly by the Word. They are so created in their freedom and dependence. While our measure is of past, present and future (and even that as we have seen is a mysterious business), for God our past, present and future is instantly contemporaneous in his new

Beginning. This is accomplished in the Divine Wisdom, Decree and Act in a way which safeguards by the Word the double contingency of creation and all within it, its own freedom and identity and nature, yet its maintenance for its being in its constant relation to God. The cost of both that freedom and that maintenance which means that in the uncreated Time of God, the new Beginning for God simultaneous with the beginning for creation which he calls forth by his Word, the Word is made flesh as the ground and fulfilment of all creation and all time. The Word takes upon himself, in his one-ness with the Father and the Spirit, incarnation, crucifixion, resurrection and ascension as the Image, the Divine Archetype of all. This is the cost of God's love towards and for creation - *the Lamb slain from the foundation of the world.*

What I am endeavouring to underline is that the event of the Word made flesh is not just first a decree of God, then something to be accomplished later. We are not concerned with a Divine Ideal only, but with an event and an accomplishment instantaneous with the decree of the Ideal. Hence Christ comes as the Beginning and the End, the Alpha and the Omega, the First and the Last.

Perhaps the narratives of the Transfiguration of Christ have this emphasis underlying them. Certainly the import of these narratives for the meaning of time in relation to Christ has been glossed over or even fundamentally ignored. Is it not that here, within our refracted time and to our veiled vision, there is glimpsed momentarily what Christ 'already' – even before his resurrection and ascension – is? The veil is lifted from human perception for a brief moment; it is an apocalyptic event irrupting into the flow of time revealing what time is in the Word's uncreated Present.

So too with the sacraments where it might be said that there is an apocalyptic import in the New Testament teaching on the matter. In Baptism we are already dead and risen with Christ and our life is hid with him in God. In the Communion – to use the old language – we are at the place where earth is bent up to heaven and heaven bent down to earth and where we join with the host of heaven in the adoration of God whose glory fills heaven and earth. The sacraments then are the 'place' where we 'see' time 'already' from the beginning of creation fulfilled in the uncreated Time of God in the Word made flesh.

If this heightened view of time fulfilled at that new Beginning for God in his uncreated Time, His dynamic Present, is permissible, then that most moving passage in Barth's work[10] takes on an even deeper meaning. He is commenting on the thirteenth and fourteenth chapters of the Gospel according to St Mark:

> All the disasters of world history, all the persecutions and trials of the community, and above all the judgement on Israel which culminates in the destruction of Jerusalem, are only the great shadow of the Cross falling on the cosmos, the Messianic woes which not even the cosmos can evade, the participation in the divine judgement effected in the death of Jesus, to which even the cosmos is subject, though this judgement is to its salvation, to the salvation of Israel, the salvation of the community, the salvation of all men, and indeed of the whole cosmos. In the cosmos in which and for which Jesus must be crucified, things can only turn out as predicted . . . Hence Jesus is primarily foretelling His own impending death when He speaks of these imminent events, and His resurrection, when to the comprehensive picture of men tormented by war, division, earthquake and famine, of the persecuted and tormented community, of Jerusalem standing under moral threat, He opposes the imminent end of time, the great καὶ τότε (and then), the coming of the Son of Man . . . The disciplines can and should look vigilantly to this future in the deep shadows lying across the world, in the afflictions of which it is threatened, in the judgements which must fall upon it, and primarily in face of the judgement of which all the other judgements are only the accompaniment, the judgement of His passion now about to commence. When all this has taken place He will come, He who now goes to destruction. He will then be revealed, He who is now shrouded in the deepest obscurity. He will triumph in judgement upon the cosmos, He who is now vanquished by the cosmos.

What this could then be seen to point to is the cost and the triumph of God in his act of creating, in that new beginning which in his dynamic Present he decides for himself, where creation and redemption are one. It could hint at the cost and triumph of the love of God in the involvement of his Being in both embracing and giving freedom to creation as the objection of that love, his stocktaking, audit and payment in the struggle with non-being which threatens and means suffering in the shadows of creation. They could show that the suffering and rejoicing which humanity and creation experience are God's in the first and primary instance, so that, for us, these become by the grace of the Word in which they are centred and recapitulate, our refracted participation in that Divine decree, act and triumph.

These are the shadows which he takes to himself at that awesomely costly Beginning in his uncreated Time and dispels them by the One who is uncreated Light, the Word, who is the Word made flesh. The interplay of disorder and order coming out of disorder, chaos and harmony coming out of chaos, are contained in the groaning and travailing and rejoicing of the birth of creation in that instant act by and in that Word, the Word made flesh. Creation is a Christological event.

8

Time and its Measurement

MEMORIAL tablets and gravestones are a good measure of what people think and believe. I do not refer to those splendidly carved and worded gargantua erected mainly in Cathedrals and large parish Churches and metropolitan burial grounds. One might consider that their elegant epitaphs would be enough to cause the departed lauded therein to blush if they could come back and stand before their graves and read. It might be considered further that it is doubtful if they were ever the recipients of such fulsome compliments from the lips and pens of those surrounding them when they were alive.

I refer rather to the humbler variety of such stones, where comparative poverty and relative obscurity necessitated bare and sparing truth rather than verbose euphemisms or flowery lies. Quite often what is commonly called the untimely death of a younger person evoked starkness of honest thought about time and its sway. One such stone, in Mouswald Churchyard, Dumfriesshire, erected to the memory of a schoolmaster, A. Bell, who died aged thirty-one on 8th January 1793, states in a few lines the relation between time and quality of existence:

> Honourable age is not that which standeth in length
> Of time,
> Nor that is measured by number of years,
> But wisdom is the gray hair unto men,
> And unspotted life is old age.

This very much echoes the Biblical idea that time is measured by the quality of its content rather than by its length. Lancelot Andrewes in the seventeenth century comments on this concept,[1] preaching on the text of Psalm 118:23, 24:

> This is the day: This? Why, are not all dayes made by Him: Is there any dayes not made by Him? Why then say we, This is the day the Lord hath made? . . . Be they faire or foule, glad or sad . . .

No difference at all, in the dayes, or in the moneths themselves. No more in November, than another moneth: not in the fifth, than in the fifteenth. All is, in God's making. For, as in the Creation, we see, all are the workes, and yet, a plaine difference betweene them for all that, in the manner of the making. Some with Sit (Let there be) ... Some with Faciamus (Let us make) with more adoe, greater forecast, and framing, as Man, that master-peece of His workes ... In the very same manner, it is with dayes; All are His making, all equal in that; but, that letteth not, but He may bestow a special Faciamus upon some one day more than other; and so, that day, by special prerogative, said To be indeed a day, that God hath made.

Now, for God's making, it fareth with dayes as it doth with yeares. Some yeare (saith the Psalme) God crowneth with His goodness, maketh it more seasonable, healthfull, fruitfull, than other. And so for dayes; God leaveth a more favourable impression of His favour, upon some one, more than many besides, by doing upon it some marvellous worke ...

As for black and dismall dayes, dayes of sorrow and sad accidents; they are and may be counted (saith Job) for no dayes; Nights rather, as having the shadow of death upon them; or, if dayes, such as his were, which Satan had marr'd, than which God had made. And for common and ordinarie dayes, wherein as there is no harm, so not any notable good, we rather say, they are gone forth from God, in the course of nature (as it were with a fiat (made), then [than] made by Him; specially, with a faciamus.

What undergirds Andrewes' observations is the concept of *order*. This term, theologically employed, comes from the biblical and Patristic statements on οἰκονομία, from which we have (though by way of narrowing of usage) our word *economy*. Originally it meant *the ordering of a household* – from which it is understandable that, given the preoccupations of our culture, we should take this over and use it merely financially, the ordering of the nation's finances, the household purse, the budgeting of the pennies in our pocket.

Its biblical and Patristic usage is grander and, while it may stoop to such preoccupations, is all inclusive. It refers primarily to the order which God is in himself; that he is pure Rationality and exists as that which is Perfect beyond our temporal understanding of perfection. This ordering is his integrity as Father and Son bound in the divine bond of love which is the Holy Spirit.

It refers secondarily to that which God creates in correspondence with the integrity of his Being – the ordering of his great
household of creation. All things, according to the Genesis
narrative and the early Christian interpretations of them in the
various patristic *Hexaemerons*, are created in order, harmony and
peace. Each field and layer of creation interacts and interlocks in
this mode with all the others in its place and in an ordered way.
All is interdependent and this is realized in the special creation of
man, the rational crown of God's creation on which is stamped,
by way of the Image of God, the Word by whom all things are
created, the image of that Rationality which God is, and to whom
the domination over all creation is committed on behalf of God.
Humanity is the final correspondence to that inital act of God in
creating light, and thereby signifiying that creation is a rational
entity.

It refers in the third place to all the activity of humanity in
that vocation and estate in which God has placed it – intellectu-
ally, morally and actively. All of which depends for its right
order on the balanced contingent relation to and from God which
is alone expressed in the One who is the Image of God by whom
all things were made and who was incarnate.

I would interject here that the fulness of this matter would lie
in what I would see as the act of God in the simultaneity of his
Present whereby the incarnation of the Word is the determinative
of creation and is, in that Present, the ordering of all time from
its inception to the end.

This ordering, which is not any form of determinism, is the
gathering up and making provision for the freedom of creation as
an entity separate from God. It is its instant fulfilment in which
we, in our respective times, participate; or rather, as the essential
corollary of this in our refracted time, we may find ourselves to
be what we are already in God, and in that light, understand (as
far as we can) and work accordingly in the freedom of our
respective spans of time and experiences that which we already
are, and have made ourselves to be, within the permission of the
order of the creative love of God.

Nor is this ordering any sort of fatalism. There can be no
laissez-faire, no *what will be will be*, in terms of our refracted time
and its measurement. There is a *what will be will be*, but only in
terms of the fact that what we are now in *our* present and have
the freedom to be now in *our* present, is already held and fulfilled

in the Present of God, gathered up in the Word made flesh. For our past is, for us, the past, but is gathered in that *Now*, in the Present of God, and our future is not yet (if it ever will be) in our *now* but is likewise already resolved in that recapitulation of the *Now* of God.

What is gathered in that Present of God is the content of our past and what will be our future. There may be the interplay of the chaos of our actions and the order in which we can only, in the propriety of what God has created us to be, live and move and have our being. There is also the interplay of chaos from circumstances and events which impinge upon us and in which we find ourselves inextricably involved, and the order of the stability which, if rationality is rationality and if creation is creation, must prevail, even if in hopelessness we cannot grasp it immediately.

This chaotic/ordered content is the substance of time. In order to explain this interplay within its widest context of Divine order and cosmic freedom, Andrewes in the genre of his age speaks of God's making and the devil's devices. And equally in the form of his time, he speaks of the overall triumph of order out of chaos, of how even the wrath of man is made to redound to the praise of God. That is the conclusion of all his sermons preached, as this one was, on the anniversary of the Gunpowder Plot, or as others were, on the anniversary of King James IV and I's deliverance from the conspiracy of the Gowrie Plot.

Theology, in its own way and in accordance with the thought forms of the particular times in which it has been expressed, deals with the relation between chaos and order. Andrewes' sermons are an example of that theological optimism which sees order even in the most confusing chaos, because such a theology looks at creation and its temporal realities through, as it were, the eyes of the crucified Christ who is also the Risen Christ. Explicitly or implicitly this sort of theology speaks of the content of time, and therefore of the quality of time. But always of time in relation to the Word made flesh – God's new Beginning in his uncreated Time made manifest in our refracted time as Jesus of Nazareth in his span of days.

It is in this context that the Hebrew thought of the Old Testament (and indeed underlying the New Testament) is concrete refracted thought par excellence. Hence because all rests in God as its fulfilment and its end, God is the 'cause' of all that befalls creation and us. In the final analysis this is so, but, as a definitive and definite statement of the relation between created existence and the Divine Being of the Creator, it bypasses the intricacies and convolutions of the double contingent relation. It is both a terrible cry and a glad acknowledgement *de profundis* and *in excelsis* from the human estate and vocation, as to where its rest is found.

The cry of dereliction from the Cross is the recapitulation of every cry from the depths of the cosmos – *My God, my God, why hast Thou forsaken me?* But this is God in the flesh who so cries out. Is not this the birth pangs of all creation in the travail of God in 'becoming' Creator? Do we not have here the shout of God in giving creation its own existence? And is not the groan and travail of all creation and the daily dilemma of our individual existence but our own echo of this?

Father into Thy hands I commend my spirit – the following and last words of the Christ in process of crucifixion – is this not the resolution of that same decision whereby all creation and time is gathered up in the integrity of its created, contingent being, into the fulness of God? And may we not understand the *It is finished* from the crucified Christ as therefore a cosmological statement of the fulfilment of all creation?

Just as each Person of the Trinity 'makes room' for the others (this is the doctrine of περιχώρησις), so that in the uncreated rationality which God is in his uncreated Time, the Father is the Father, the Son the Son and the Spirit the Spirit, without confusion yet nevertheless one in the bond of divine Love, so in creating by the Word, God 'makes room' for us in our created dimension. We may call time the 'place' granted by God as the created dimension whereby we are what we are. It is the place where we live and move and have our being in our contingent relation with God. How we live in the freedom of this dimension in that contingent relation amid all the relativity of the orders of creation, is that which determines the quality of our existence. We are concerned with time, therefore, as quality in the first instance.

The measurement of time is of secondary consideration, albeit a necessary convenience. The mistake is to think of time merely in terms of measurement, and that it is in its measurement only that time exists.

It is through such thought that the nature of time becomes

veiled because of the ultimate inability of the human mind to cope with its – to us – infinite span. Having been accorded the status of such a mystery, time begins to exercise a tyranny over us. The servant becomes the master and the master the slave.

St Augustine tackles the problem of the nature of time and the measurement of time in book XI of the *Confessions*. He introduces this with the question[2]

> Is it possible, O Lord, that, since thou art in eternity, thou art ignorant of what I am saying to thee? Or, dost thou see in time an event at the time it occurs? If not, then why am I recounting such a tale of things to thee?

In this question, the dilemma of our contact with God, of created time with 'eternity' and of how we can understand God to perceive time, is laid out succinctly. He betrays his view of time as having a ceaseless passage in an aside:[3]

> . . . the drops of time are precious to me.

The reference here is to that means of measuring time with which he would be familiar, the *clepsydra*, the water clock. But this passage of time is in the control of God:[4]

> At thy bidding the moments fly.

He makes the point strongly that ordinary human words are made and heard in time – the syllables sound and pass away. How then did God speak when it is recounted that God said 'Let the heaven and earth be made'? If there is not an absolute distinction between this speech of God with its production, and ordinary words, then[5]

> If . . . in words that sound and fade away thou didst say that heaven and earth should be made, and thus madest heaven and earth, then there was already some kind of corporeal creature before heaven and earth by whose motions in time that voice might have had its occurence in time. But there was nothing corporeal before the heavens and the earth; or if there was, then it is certain that already, without a time-bound voice, thou hadst created whatever it was out of which thou didst make the time-bound voice by which thou didst say, 'Let the heaven and the earth be made!'

Augustine elaborates on the necessity of perceiving that God speaks 'eternally' in his eternal Word, and in so doing he implies

that God's 'eternity' is an uncreated Present and that all things
are created instantaneously, yet apparently goes on to contradict
himself in the matter[6]:

> Thou dost call us, then, to understand the Word – the God who
> is God with thee – which is spoken eternally. For what was first
> spoken was not finished, and then something else spoken until the
> whole series was spoken; but all things at the same time and
> forever. For, otherwise, we should have time and change and not
> a true eternity, not a true immortality ... And, therefore, unto
> the Word co-eternal with thee, at the same time and always thou
> sayest all that thou sayest. And whatever thou sayest shall be
> made is made, and thou makest nothing otherwise than by
> speaking. Still, not all the things that thou dost make by speaking
> are made at the same time and always.

The last quoted sentence is no doubt added as a qualification
in case what he had stated before could be deduced as a doctrine
of the eternity of the world. So careful is he in this matter
throughout his observations that this sort of qualification probably lies behind Grosseteste's later pondering as to why Augustine
was not forthright on the matter of the simultaneity of all
creation.[7]

If we look at what Augustine says, before he adds his rider
for safety's sake, there is an important element, often overlooked,
concerning the mode of creation. God speaks in silence; only a
time-bound voice can be heard. That is to say, the conversation of
God and the creative edict, issues within that existence which
God is in himself. This speech is unique to God alone and heard
by God alone, for it is a speech of the God who alone exists
'eternally'. The Father and the Word converse in the Spirit and
thus it is conversation and a decree which is beyond comparison
and silently imperceivable to any *time-bound* mode of communica-
tion. It is only a matter of revelation that we can hear this and
comprehend it as far as our *time-bound* perception allows. It is
only by our hearing of that incomprehensible Word made flesh
that we can hear the *Let there be* ... *Let us make* and appreciate
the mode of creation.

It is this Word, also carefully noted by Augustine[8] in order
to lay the ground of his following argument, to be *thy Son, thy
Power, thy Wisdom, thy Truth*, by whom all things are created.
This self-same Word or Wisdom is the Beginning in whom God
has made heaven and earth. This concept of Beginning, Augustine

now elaborates by way of answering the question placed as a conundrum by the Manichees whom he was combating.[9]:

> 'What was God doing before he made heaven and earth? for if He was idle,' they say, 'and did nothing, then why did he not continue in that state for ever – doing nothing, as he had always done? If any new motion has arisen in God, and a new will to form a creature, which he had never before formed, how can that be a true eternity in which an act of will occurs that was not there before? . . . The will of God . . . pertains to His every Essence. Yet if anything has arisen in the Essence of God that was not there before, then that Essence cannot truly be called eternal. But if it was the eternal will of God that creation should come to be, why, then, is not the creation itself also from eternity?'

Augustine's answer is that the Manichees are incapable of understanding the difference between temporal existence and measurement and the Divine Existence. The latter they compare with temporal processes. It may be noted that here Augustine was faced with a parallel problem to that of Athanasius with the Arians, and that there is equally a parallel response regarding time and its beginning compared to that new Beginning in God, which necessitated in both cases an interpretation of that concept of Beginning which was shown not to compromise the non-temporal nature of God.

Augustine then goes on to emphasise that 'eternity' is not endless time. The Manichees fail to appreciate that a long time is only long because of the number of separate events which occur in its passage, and that these are successive and not simultaneous, for no temporal process is simultaneous.[10]

> In the Eternal, on the other hand, nothing passes away, but the whole is simultaneously present . . . Therefore let it [that is the unstable heart of those who fail to perceive the qualitative difference between time and 'eternity'] see that all time past is forced to move on by the incoming future [note the hint of time as the movement of water again]; that all the future follows from the past; and that all, past and future is created and issues out of that which is forever present. Who will hold the heart of man that it may stand still and see how the eternity which always stands still is itself neither future nor past but expresses itself in the times that are future and past?

Augustine reports the answer of one to those who had asked

'What as God doing before he created heaven and earth?' as 'he was preparing hell for those who ask too deep'. His rather pious dismissal of this, that it is one thing to see the answer and another to laugh at the questioner, and that he himself would not answer such in this way, may well be right, but shows his lack of a sense of humour. His answer is that there could not be unnumbered ages where God did nothing, for this would presuppose a temporal medium, and God is the maker of all the ages. How could such ages have not been made by God? There could be no time before he made time: God does not precede any period of time by another period of time, for he sets the temporal procession in being.[11]

> Thy years neither go nor come; but ours both go and come in order that all separate moments may come to pass. All thy years stand together as one, since they are abiding. Nor do thy years past exclude the years to come because thy years do not pass away. All these years of ours shall be with thee, when all of them shall have ceased to be. Thy years are but a day, and thy day is not recurrent, but always today. Thy 'today' yields not to tomorrow and does not follow yesterday. Thy 'today' is eternity. Therefore thou didst generate the Coeternal, to whom thou didst say, 'This day I have begotten thee'. Thou madest all time and before all times thou art, and there was never a time when there was no time.

What Augustine means by the last observation is that time is an entity in itself; it is not 'eternity' or God's Present. He does not mean that it is itself eternal. It comes into being as time, it does not come into being as a span in some endless time. Time is simply time and there can be no time outside it.

The tenor of the whole argument is that we cannot solve the question of the relation of God's uncreated Existence as uncreated Time by the application of our measurement of time. Time itself is only measured by its passing, by its direction from the past to the future. But even this is problematical when it comes to attempting to describe what time is. We assume that we know what it is when left to ourselves in our self thoughts. We talk about it familiarly as if we knew all about it. But if we are asked directly – then we find we do not know about time. All that we can know (and this passage would surely gladden the hearts of the authors of *The Arrow of Time*) is from its direction.[12]

... I say with confidence that I know that if nothing passed away, there would be no past time; and if nothing were still coming, there would be no future time; and if there were nothing at all, there would be no present time.

But, then, how is it that there are two times, past and future, when even the past is now no longer and the future is now not yet? But if the present were always present, and did not pass into past time, it obviously would not be time but eternity. If, then, time present – if it be time – comes into existence only because it passes into time past, how can we say that even this IS, since the cause of its being is that it will cease to be? Thus, can we not truly say that time IS only as it tends toward nonbeing?

Augustine is arguing here that time does not exist as a measurable entity. That is not to say that it does not exist, only that its existence eludes being typified and qualified by measurement. We only speak in terms of 'long' and 'short' with regard to the past and the future. A hundred years is long in comparison to ten days in that which is past or in that which is to come. But how can that which has non-existence be long or short. The past has gone; the future is not yet. It cannot be right to say 'it is long' with regard to past or future time. For the past 'it was long' would be more correct. Yet even here we are in a quandary. Past time was a passing of successive moments. They could not be long or short for they were passing, and as they momentarily passed ceased to be long.

He emphasises this elusiveness of time. We cannot even describe the present. We cannot say that a hundred years are present. Nor is a year, nor a day, nor an hour, nor any of the fleeting fractions which we arrive at when we divide and subdivide our measurements. The present flies so rapidly from the future to the past that it cannot be discerned, caught and quantified.

Yet he seems to take a step backwards from what he has been generally describing, as though to save himself from the seemingly unavoidable conclusion that time has no reality and that the present is an illusion[13]:

But we measure the passage of time when we measure the intervals of perception. But who can measure times past which are no longer, or times future which are not yet – unless perhaps someone will dare to say that what does not exist can be measured?

> Therefore, while time is passing, it can be perceived and measured.

Yet he had previously stated as the conclusion of an involved argument that[14]:

> But the present has no extension whatsoever.

But this is not a saving-face statement. There is more to it than that. Although the tenor of his statement seems to suggest that he is talking about the measurement of the present (and in such a understandable interpretation lies the charge of his apparent contradiction), he is writing of the measuring of the passage of time, as he later makes explicit in XI:27. For Augustine there is an arrow of time – but (and here most importantly for what he might have progressed towards) he perceives the direction of time not as moving forward into the future, but rather flowing from the future into the past. That is to say, it comes from the future and in a fleeting immeasurable moment, is past.

The importance of this is a key statement for an understanding of what he is trying to say about time. He begins with what he was taught as a youth – that there are three times, past, present and future. Can the past and the future exist, despite all that is said? The past is past and gone, the future is not yet and unknowable. Does only the present exist? Yet, is it not that[15]:

> ... when, from the future, time becomes present, it proceeds from some secret place; and when, from times present, it becomes past, it recedes into some secret place?

Where is that place? he asks.[16] Then, tantalizingly does not give any definite direction towards an answer. He merely states that wherever they are, the future is there as 'not yet' and as the past as 'no longer' and so wherever they are and whatever they are, they are there not as future and past but as present.

Had he gone on here at this stage in his developing argument to say that they are in the Present of God and embraced by it, then a whole dimension of thought would have been opened out.

But as it is, this is only an entrance into the way he takes by 'psychologizing' the matter. In taking this way, he enlarges on the fact that his childhood is present to him in his mind; that in his mind, seeing the first rays of dawn, the sun rises though it has

not yet come above the horizon. Thus, past, present and future
are present in the mind.[17]

> Perhaps it may be said rightly that there are three times, past,
> present, and future: a time present of things past; a time present
> of things present; and a time present of things future. For these
> three coexist somehow in the soul, for otherwise I could not see
> them. The time present of things past is memory; the time
> present of things present is direct experience; the time present of
> things future is expectation. If we are allowed to speak of these
> things so, I see three times, and I grant that there are three . . .
> always provided that what is said is understood, so that neither
> the future nor the past is said to exist now.

He subjectivizes the whole issue, and in the end denies that
time is separable from the mind. It only exists as imaginative
reflection or expectation. It must be asked if this does not side-
step the whole issue. This becomes even more subjective as he
goes on to return to and deal with the measurement of time.
He restates the problem of measuring the past which has gone,
the future which is not yet and the present which is too fleeting.
So how is the measurement achieved and in what does it consist?
The answer Augustine gives is that it is measured in and by the
mind.[18]

> It is in you, O mind of mine, that I measure the periods of time.
> Do not shout me down that it exists [objectively]; do not over-
> whelm yourself with the turbulent flood of your impressions. In
> you, as I said, I measure the periods of time. I measure as time
> present the impressions things make on you as they pass by and
> what remains after they have passed by – I do not measure the
> things themselves which have passed by and left their impression
> on you. This is what I measure when I measure periods of time.
> Either then, these are the periods of time or else I do not measure
> time at all . . . Who denies that time present has no length, since
> it passes away in a moment? Yet, our attention has a continuity
> and it is through this that what is present may proceed to become
> absent. Therefore, future time, which is non-existent, is not long;
> but 'a long future' is 'a long expectation of the future'. Nor is
> time past, which is no longer, long; a 'long past' is 'a long
> memory of the past'.

There is a correct emphasis in the writings of Augustine which
underlines the fact that existence and time are bound together.
But two observations must be made: first, that we must not
confuse time with the measurement of time, and, second, that if

we exist in refracted time we cannot deduce the nature of time from our observation and qualifying of its passage. We require a vantage point to view time as totality, and to see the quality of time as it passes for us in the light of that total context.

It is the entrance of God as uncreated Time into our created time which provides this vantage point as far as theology's statement about time is concerned. We can only know time in its totality there, where it is recapitulate and where the End has been joined to the Beginning and the whole sweep of the epic of creation is uttered in the one Word of God. Time in its totality is bound up with the existence of the uncreated Word of God become a word of man, and creation seen in its contingent relation to and from its Creator. It is at the point where incarnation and creation are seen to be the one instant act of God in his uncreated Time, that the unfolding of created time and its quality for individual existence and all created existence can become apparent. The realization of time as that which is in its totality present in the Present of God but as that which is refracted for us in our created existence, provides the necessary balance where the objective and the subjective views of time are held together.

If, as Augustine suggests, a subjective understanding of time is all in all, this can only lead ultimately to either the horror of the individual being time's captive, and to that determinism which is all too apparent in his doctrine of double Predestination, or the the equally fearsome idea that time is what we make it, again which equally is apparent in the individualism underlying Augustine's theology of salvation. (Here, it may be added, it is no surprise that appeal has been and is made constantly to Augustine by the adherents of both sides of Protestant eccentricity, its fatalistic side and its intense preoccupation with individual salvation).

To say that time is 'all in the mind', is to confuse a subjective judgment about the measurement of time – whether it appears long or short to the individual in his or her experiences – with time itself. Equally, we have to see that this is one element in how we look at time, for it does indicate this profound understanding of the unity between existence and time. But the solution does not lie in the consideration of our existence as that which we experience as created entities.

It must go farther than this, and point to the relation of time in its contingency to and from the Existence of God where all time is held in his creative and incarnate act in Christ. Our time can only be seen and measured in that Time of Jesus Christ, that is, the creative decree and conversation and act of God which is an Instant in the Present of the Trinity.

The mystery of our time is how it is refracted into our past, 'present' and future, yet is fulfilled as that Present Instant in Christ. All other explanations can only be on the basis of 'three-dimensional absurdities', and it is the consideration of these, when we fall in to them, which cause us to turn them into more entangled and contradictory mysteries.

Let one example of such suffice: the tangle into which people entwine themselves when arguing about time and ghosts. Do ghosts come back to us in our time, or are we transported back to their time? This, of course, presupposes that there is such a phenomenon as a ghost, but apart from that and more importantly, it reveals the fact that there is little understanding of time except on the basis of a belief that it is as a straight line which may fold back or forward on itself. There is generally no understanding of time as a totality in such arguments.

In considering Augustine's statements about time in his *Confessions*, we cannot ignore his assertion that time comes from the future and goes into the past. This might seem to suggest that he is speaking of an arrow of time which indicate a movement of time from the right to the left, so to speak. The more general consensus seem to be that it does the opposite and moves from the past towards the future, from the left to the right, as it were.

The authors of *The Arrow of Time* are explicit about their beliefs from the field of scientific proof[19]: that the direction of time, as an arrow, points from the past to the future. They say that this common-sense view of time is advocated eloquently in the field of literature, where there is often expressed that life has an irreversible end which cannot be recalled, and its span is but short. The ineluctable progress of time heightens for the literary person, the intensity and poignancy of each moment of life – every moment to be savoured and treasured – and the very ephemerality of our existence adds to its essential mystery. All this is sharpened by the knowledge of coming death.

The irreversibility of time, and its partitioning as past, 'present' and future, is set out by scientific argument in all that follows in that work. It is not for me, or any theologian, to take issue on scientific grounds with such an argument. Indeed the book persaudes and commands the assent to this irreversibility as fact. It is not with the fact that one wishes to take issue, or with the proofs leading to the fact. But it is a matter of question as to whether or not the phrase *The Arrow of Time* could be misleading.

I ask if it is but a partial statement, for it seems to be that whether we say that time comes from the future and goes into the past, or that there is a flow of time which goes, as *The Arrow of Time* argues, from the past to the future, we speak of the same irreversibility – namely that the past is past and cannot be resurrected. It is done, over and final. But beneath this, is there not a fuller question – 'Whence comes time and whither does it go?' The phrase *The Arrow of Time* is admirably suited to indicate the irreversibility of time – but only on the created dimension of the recognition of past and future.

If time comes and moves, and if it is purposeful and has rationality, it must have a source and an end, from which and in which its purpose and rationality is declared and fulfilled. Otherwise it is meaningless, and therefore existence, as existence in time, is meaningless. Is this not the *secret place* of Augustine? And, instead of reverting into subjectivism, is it not a pity that his essentially static view of 'eternity' did not allow him to follow up his statement that *In the eternal . . . nothing passes away, but the whole is simultaneously present?*

Measurement of time, or rather, a consideration of its quality, must have to do with this beginning and end. The contention of theology might be that as the Creator Word made flesh is the Beginning and the End, the First and the Last, in the creative act of God, then time is measured by the measure of Christ. Time's movement is under the compulsion of the Word of God, who is the Beginning and the End, the Alpha and Omega. Time's substance is that which is contingent to and from the One who is all time, for he is uncreated Present. Time is therefore primarily and finally a Christological event.

9

Time, Place and Existence

AUGUSTINE regards the future and the past as coming from and going to a secret place.[1] That time should proceed from a secret place and recede into a secret place is a concept which he did not develop. Instead, as is outlined above, he removes the whole question of the procession of time and its measurement as it proceeds, into the realm of the mental awareness of the individual. But time has its place.

Time and space are inextricably united. They are the dimensions of this order in which we live and move and have our being. They are not, however, as Newton would have it, a rigid, mathematical framework, an inert absolute, which is co-terminous – though not identical – with the eternity and infinity of God, into which existence is fitted, and to which measurable, observable time and space in the motion of created bodies, were to be referred.

The danger is, of course, that it is all too small a jump to identify God in his 'eternity' and 'infinity' with absolute time and space, and fall into he idea that in the last resort the creation is therefore eternal and infinite. Newton himself safeguarded against this, for he is clear in the *General Scholium* that God is not identifical with eternity and infinity, with absolute time and space. Nevertheless, there is a fine proximation and an over-similarity.

For Newton, it is the absolute which imparts and indeed mechanically determines the rationality of the relative. This theory, magnificent as it may have been in its construction and application, is at the heart Aristotelian. Although much of Aristotelian physics was overturned by Newton, this is, nevertheless, but a modification of the 'receptacle' theory of Aristotle, in which space (and therefore time) is seen as the receptacle which contains all things. For Newton it was impossible that God, who is regarded as inflexible and unmoving like absolute time and space, should become man. For how could that which contains by absolute time and space become a part of that which is contained? This is why Newton in the last resort could not accept the Incarnation.

We have here, despite Newton's insistence that creation was a creation *ex nihilo*, out of nothing, and despite his desire to link creation to God via absolute and infinite space and time, a basic dualism between God and creation, between the absolute and the corporeal, between form and content. It may be a fact that Newton's theories can be scientifically criticized and, from the point of theology, seen as laying the foundations (even if Newton would have protested at the idea) of later rationalist deism. Yet, I would wish to point out that at least his intent should be salvaged.

That intent is surely his realization that God comprehends all time and space. Newton's refusal (though this was not carried out to the measure of the zeal of his statements on the matter) to construct hypotheses, and his insistence on deductive reasoning and analytical mathematics, blinded him to any consideration of a dynamic God to and from whom creation had a living contingent relation. A statically mathematical approach to time and space precluded any notion in his mind that time and space are the existence of all that is; they are a description of the character and nature of a creation contingent to and from God in and through and by his Creator Word. Yet surely the desire to see all time and space related to God is there.

The state of scientific and theological awareness at that time had been pushed on to a path of philosophical presupposition strewn with the sprouting seeds of a rising dualistic deism. Such was that growth, that they bypassed the opportunity for the rediscovery and reconsideration of that emphasis which had been stated in the works of the Greek Fathers, re-surfaced in Grosseteste and Duns Scotus and re-stated in some of the theological and scientific works of the sixteenth and early seventeenth centuries (particularly those of Calvin and Francis Bacon). It is therefore perhaps unfair to blame Newton (no doubt as unattractive figure and an opportunist of some dubiety in professional etiquette, as Stephen Hawking points out[2]). His achievement, given the inclination of his times, was monumental (even if it was not all of his own originality).

The failure to relate time, place and being, led to far-reaching and lingering mechanistic interpretations of all aspects of existence – not least in principles governing what is called 'the social sciences' – and deeply entrenched attitudes which can lead to what may be seen to be malevolent technology and the emphasis on man as *homo faber* to the exclusion of the part the humanities have to play in the formation of human growth. It even influenced the philosophy of history, as may be instanced by the frameworks set up as norms of historical judgment by 'whig' or 'liberal' historians in the mould of MacAulay and, later, H. A. L. Fisher. History has had its own battles to fight on this score, and the insistence of R. G. Collingwood on interpreting facts within the norms and contexts of their times (inasfar as such could be understood), rather than in the light of an idealized framework of culture values, is an instant of that dispute.

As we have already noted, we would rather say that time is a 'co-creation',[3] that is, it is that which becomes along with all that is, as a product of existence, a corollary of creation. Creation is the place of time. In what way, then, is this placed time related to the 'time' and 'place' of God?

Straightaway, let us put aside any idea of absolute time and absolute space, however laudable Newton's intent may have been to use such a concept as a means of relating creation and time to God. When we speak of God's 'time' and 'place', we are in the realms of necessitous care in employing such terminology. God is not the sum, or the highest instance, of all time and space. We have spoken before of God's 'time'[4] as uncreated Time, trying (as far as the limitations of time-bound language will permit) to describe it as a Dynamic Present, such as we cannot experience in the flow of time in which we live out our created existence. We noted then, and re-emphasise now, that such terms as 'time' and 'place' when applied to God, are entirely inappropriate if used indiscriminately or promiscuously. Each term has to be bent out of its normal use of application to created entities and their circumstances, and regarded in a way which allows the qualitative distinction between God and creation to recast it. It has to be employed in a way and with a new meaning which is faithful to the Nature of the Object it is serving.

We may approach this problem by first noting that it is entirely wrong to speak of the Incarnation (which must always be our vantage point in our looking for God) as 'God *in* time'– as erroneous as saying that Christ is 'God *in* man'. The Incarnation is God arising out of his 'place' to take man's place to himself; it is God with his uncreated Time, his Present, assuming man's time into union with himself by taking that created time into himself. God comes *as* man, *as* time, *as* man's place.

He comes, taking such to himself, without forsaking his Time, his Place, his Godness. Indeed it is the last, his Godness, which is his Time and Place. As in the created dimension, time and place is existence and existence is place and time, so in the uncreatedness of God, his uncreated Existence is his Time and his Place. There is no such thing, we have to underline again, as 'eternity' as a dimension which happens to be inhabited by a Being suitable to exist in its 'dimensions'. This is so too of the created sphere. There is no such thing as time and place independent of created existence, which happen to be peopled and filled with entities commensurate with the dimensions and nature of time and space. The existence and nature of these created entities are time and space, for time and space are the expression of that existence and nature.

We are accustomed in popular usage to speak of 'someone in his or her time'. This betrays how entrenched in our thought the container theory of time and place is. *God's in His heaven – All's right with the world*[5] is another instance of this mode of thinking.

This may be deemed to be close to the subjectivism of Augustine which has been criticized already. But, on the contrary, it is an expression of the unity of all creation which is created time, from that beginning to its end. That is our time and place – the time and place which all creation is, into which we fit in our interdependent and interlocking existences. Time is as rich as the variety of created entities which have been, are, and will be.

It is perhaps easier to see this with regard to place. A place is recognizable by that assortment and disposition of created entities in their relation to one to another and to all. Place is not a theoretical vacuum, a formal shell and things fitted within its compass. A place is either beautiful or drab, comfortable or desolate and so on. But it is the things perceived which make it so for us. Moreover, a place may appear as home to one and alien to another Those contrary subjective assessments do not alter the actuality of the constitution of that place, any more than preference for mountains raises up the plain or love of flat panoramas levels the high places. We may, it goes without saying, seek to alter a place to suit our tastes which have already been formed for familiarity with and appreciation of, other places, and therefore it may become an altered place. But place it remains.

So with time. We may seek 'to spend our time' in one way or another. What this really means is to 'dispose our existence' in such a way that it is either creative or resting; productive or whiled away, and so on. But all this refers to our existence and only by extension to time. So time will appear long or short, wearisome or happy – but it is not time which is this or that, but our disposition primarily. Such biblical phrases as *the times of our disobedience* refer primarily to the existence of our fracturing our contingency to and from God and therefore our denial of the fundamental nature of our existence.

In our refracted existence, the created dimension, time, place and existence appear as divorced, and we tend to live on the assumption that they are. It is only with God that his Time, his Place and his Existence are one. That is why Athanasius forcibly notes that it was wrong of the Arian heretics to ask 'Is God in place?', for this presupposes a disjunction between God and his 'eternity', assuming that 'eternity' is a dimension independent of God. There can be no such tension with God. He is his Place and his Time.

But even if we make distinctions on the created level between time, place and our existence, nevertheless there is a distinct correlation between time, place and existence. For example, there is a relation between the time as regarded as trying, something to be endured, and persons 'out of place'. 'How long, O Lord, how long?' is the cry of the displaced person longing for the right orientation between himself and his surroundings and circumstances. The individual in dull employment where his or her skills and qualities are not realized or utilized properly, experiences the dragging out of time. Yet it is the uncongenial work which is the cause, the incompatability of the individual and the employment, not time by itself as it were a separate entity independent of place and existence. Or again, someone may be described as being 'born before his time', or like St Paul's autobiographical comment, *as . . . one born out of due time.*[6] This refers to the experience or the achievement of the individual's existence in the context of those persons and circumstances which surround him. That is, underlying the terminology using time, there is an unconscious recognition of place and existence too.

Even farther underneath, there is an implicit assumption of the unity of time in its bond with place and existence. There is something poignant and evocative in the aspect of an ancient ruin, or a dwelling which has remained in its original state for centuries. Place, the same now as it was, seems to telescope the sense of time and make, even if nebulously, the existence of the persons of generations past, contemporary. The opposite is also true, when the surroundings of a childhood changed by the hand of the 'developer' causes the pain of the awareness of the gulf of passing years.

Such common experiences and phraseology, because they are the awareness and expressions of being, often reveal an intuitive grasp of this bond between time and place and existence. They are not to be dismissed as the merely subjective and statements of subjective attitudes. In any case, they are far from being the whole truth of the matter. Equally, they can reveal the ideas long accepted through the permeation of mistaken tenets of high philosophy down to the ground level of common usage – 'in time', as a manifestation of some measure of Aristotelian residue deeply embedded in popular outlook formed, in the first instance, by various philosophic, scientific and theological media, being a case in point.

But such common experiences and statements are not to be disregarded as of no import in a study of the nature of time. The two sides of such – the intuitive and the false assumptions – when disentangled can be most revealing as to the relation of time and place and person.

There is a co-relating of these three, time and place and existence, in the Niceno-Constantinopolitan Creed. The hinterland of dispute with the Arians in their confusion of the created and the uncreated dimensions, led to carefully considered and precisely worded statements on the matter by the Nicene Fathers of the fourth century.

The language of the Creed, while it is certainly the language of devotion and worship, springs from that which gives rise to devotion and worship – the self-revelation of God. The terminology is bent out of its normal day-by-day usage to serve the reality and integrity of the nature of that self-revelation. When we look at the references to place, the spatial concepts, to time, the temporal concepts, or to existence, the Persons of Father, Son and Holy Spirit, enshrined in the Creed, we find that none of these are divorced from the others. Space, time and existence are not regarded in isolation from one another, but form an overall unity in the Creed. This existence/place/time unity centres on and springs from the existence of the Word made flesh.

The Creed begins with a statement:

> . . . God, the Father Almighty, Maker of heaven and earth, and of all things visible and invisible.

This is the theological assertion of the transcendence of God over all space and time, for these are the co-creations of his creative decree and act in bringing all things into existence *ex nihilo*. There is no thought here of a spatial relation between God and creation. Creation is not related to God as the limited to the absolute, as measurable space to infinite space, as a created place to a heavenly place.

The Word of God, is described as

> Light from Light, Very God of Very God, Begotten not made, being of one substance with the Father, by Whom all things were made. Who for us men and for our salvation, came down from heaven. And was incarnate . . .

The primary concentration is on the Triune, uncreated existence of God, the unity of the Father with the Son, the interior and 'eternal' relations within God's 'Godness'. It is this relationship of the Father to the Son and the Son to the Father which is the principle of relation to creation. This is the importance of the ὁμοούσιος, *homoousios* – the *of one substance* clause, expressing the Godness of the Son as one with the Godness of the Father. The Son is God as is the Father, and it is by decree of the Father that the Son creates. There is no disjunction or disparity in the unity of the Father's existence with the existence of the Son, and yet the integrity of the Person of the Son and the integrity of the Person of the Father is not compromised.

The way in which the early Church came to formulate the realization of the doctrine of the Trinity in the fourth century was to see the Father as 'making room' for the Son and the Son for the Father. This 'making room' [περιχώρησις] is the work and role, and indeed the existence, of the Holy Spirit. This was not a spatial statement, but an expression of the mode of existence of the Father and the Son in the bond of Divine Love, the Holy Spirit. It refers to the dynamic relation of love within the Triunity of God, the total unity in the diversity of Persons.

Here the phrase 'making room for' has been bent out of its common usage and application, and made to refer to something qualitatively different than mere spatial measurement.

When it is said that the Son *came down from heaven*, again this is not a statement of his voyaging movement from one place to another, from a higher to a lower dimension, in spatial terms. It concerns the existence of the uncreated Word who takes created existence to himself in the Incarnation, and who 'makes room for' creation in taking it into unity his Divine existence, without disjunction and without compromise to the integrity of the created dimension and his Divine existence. That is not to say that he does not really come as man. It does say that while so doing, he remains the Creator Word, still upholding as to his Divine Nature, all creation.

What may appear as a rather obscure and unnecessary debate on this matter in the late sixteenth century, between the Calvinists and the Lutherans, is, in fact of much import. The Lutherans (influenced much by Aristotelian philosophy), still regarded space or place as a 'container'. So concerned were they for the unity of God and man in Christ, that they regarded the Word of God in all his Divine Nature being 'poured' into his human nature. This had the effect of localizing the Word, of containing the Creator Word. The Calvinists correctly questioned this in terms of 'how did he then oversee all creation if he was so contained?' Their point was that while still remaining God, the Lord and upholder of all things, he became man. The Lutherans countered this by dubbing such a statement the *Extra Calvinisticum*, the *Calvinistic Extra*. That is, they interpreted this to mean that something of the Word must have been left 'extra', or outside the humanity of Christ.

This illustrates the preposterous difficulties which arise if terminology of space and time is not bent out of its normal usage when applied to God and the things of God. We cannot apportion God according to the measuring standards whereby we deal with the created dimension. The difference is one of quality, not quantity, and the difficulty is to cleanse terms of their necessary quantitative meaning in order that they may point to a qualitative distinction. While we may desire to stress the reality of the place of the Incarnation, and therefore the reality of the humanity of Christ, we cannot so localize God. Great care has to be exercised in the choice and employment of terms as pointers to that which is beyond the limit of human comprehension and capability of expression.

Such terms and concepts as were employed by the Nicene Fathers in the Creed were seen by them to be demanded, formed and controlled by the compelling reality of that which confronted them – the full significance of the Word made flesh as it unfolded from the biblical witnesses to the Person and event of Jesus Christ. The Patristic mind was – as indeed the theological mind must be – the biblical mind. The terminology the Nicene Fathers employed was essentially biblical, even the ὁμοούσιος clause, disputed because as such it is not found in Scripture, being eventually accepted and included as being in the general spirit of Scipture's meaning with regard to the relation of the Son to the Father.

The resulting Creed is a distillation of Scripture, concentrating the biblical witness with clarity and precision, and giving an overall interpretation. Its terminology was carved out carefully as being a series of pointers faithful to the nature of the Person of Christ who was regarded as the σκοπός, the 'scope' in the sense of *horizon, substance, goal* of Scripture. This, of course, is opposed to any idea that the truth of the matter can be read instantly, automatically and mechanically from the written words of the Bible. This denies the paradeigmatic nature of Scripture and assumes that the Bible is the 'container' of God.

The paradeigmatic nature of Scripture, pointing to the Divine reality beyond itself, is also the hallmark of Credal statements. Temporal and spatial words used as appertaining to God, are bent out of their normal use and emptied of their created time and space content. Otherwise the created dimension is projected into God who then is regarded as the highest instance of what we experience and know here.

Such spatial and temporal terms, however, when they refer to the humanity of Christ, his existence in time, are treated differently, for then they rightly convey a temporal and spatial content. We may, for example refer to the 'pierced hands of Christ on the cross'. 'Hand' here is an ordinary, familiar and immediately understood term. But when we refer, as Irenaeus constantly did, to the Word and the Spirit as *the hands of God* in creating, then the term has a different usage. It refers to the Personal loving involvement and skill with which God creates; it does not seek to portray him as an infinitely extended version of an ingenious human craftsman.

The two usages of terminology come together when applied to Christ. There is the usage of conveying the reality of the dimension of time and things by Scripture and Creed when they refer to the datable, observable, tangible, humanity of Christ, who was born, hungered, thirsted, was tempted, spoke and taught, suffered under Pontius Pilate, was crucified, died and was buried, rose again and ascended. Yet this particular entity and dimension as a human reality is also the reality of God. That Divine reality is attested in such phraseology as *ascended into heaven, seated at the right hand of God the Father almighty, whose kingdom shall have no end*. The mistake is a failure to distinguish between their respective applications, which are determined by the dimension to which they are seeking to point.

Even if the Ascension is treated as a removal upwards in the disciples' sight, as a sign given, yet its essentially non-natural usage is confirmed by the biblical observation that *a cloud received him from their sight*.[7] *Cloud* in biblical terminology, in both the Old and New Testaments, is the sign used to denote the indescribable glory and mystery of God. In other words, Christ removes to that realm which is 'over' and 'beyond' and 'above' the discerning and comprehension of the mind. He removes from this place to his Divine 'Place', yet his human place here in the time on his earthly existence is also his Divine 'Place' in his Incarnation, and in his Ascension his Divine 'Place' is also the place of his humanity in which he rose in Resurrection. It is this union between the human and the Divine which means a union between creation and its place and Creator and Divine 'Place'. It also means a union between created time and God's 'Time'.

The observations of some Patristic theology on the mode of union of the two natures of Christ at the Incarnation, his human nature and his Divine nature, hold a clue to possible applications to the nature of time. These particular observations revolve round two Greek words, ἀνυπόστασις (*anhupostasis*) and ἐνυπόστασις (*enhupostasis*). Ὑπόστασις (*hupostasis*) means 'mode of being'; ἀν – *apart from*; ἐν – *in*. *Anhupostasis* emphasises the negative assertion about the humanity of Christ. 'Apart from' its union with the mode of existence of the Divine Word, it has no existence of its own. It is '*anhupostatic*'. *Enhupostasis* underlines the positive assertion about the human nature of Christ, 'In' its union with the mode of existence of the Eternal Word, it has an existence of its own. It is *enhupostatic*.

This may be put in this way, clumsy as it may read: the human nature of Jesus Christ has no being or mode of existence apart from its being in union with the being and mode of existence of the Eternal Word, and, conversely, the human being of Jesus Christ has real existence and mode of existence in its union with the being and mode of existence of the Eternal Word.

This rules out (amongst other things which are not necessary for our consideration here) the idea that Jesus Christ was a man adopted by God to be his son, that he had an independent human existence of his own and at a given point in his life was chosen to be so. Rather it safeguards the true union of the two natures in their respective integrities by setting out the relation between them in that union and thus safeguarding the ineffable truth that this Jesus Christ is both the uncreated Word of God in all his Godness and human in all the reality of that created being. It therefore underlines that this Jesus Christ is the entrance of the created into the uncreated without dissolving that essential, ineffable, incomprehensible mystery which God is to all created entities.

The time of Jesus Christ is therefore the time which God has for us and makes for us in taking humanity, that is the rationale of all creation, into his Divinity and giving it existence there. The time of Jesus Christ is God's human existence for us in which he makes room in his Divine existence for the dimension of creation. God's time for us is the existence of the man Jesus, and as such, as we have already stressed, he is the fulness of time.

We are therefore faced with looking at the possibility of a qualitatively graded contingency when speaking about the nature of time. For it is the same as that contingency on which all existence rests. We live and move and have our being in this created dimension. But we do so as contingent to that humanity of Christ in its union with the Word of God and wherein we find our contingency from him as distinct and individual beings. That humanity of his is itself contingent to the Word who gives it existence in creating it in union with himself and giving it contingency from, in that it has its identity and individuality. But this identity and individuality is unlike the identity and

individuality of any other human being because of its union with
the Divine. Christ is Person in a unique way.

The concept 'person' has to be understood at this point. It is
used normally to indicate self-sufficient, self-determined and
self-conscious individuality. Its theological use, both of God and
of humanity, is different.

T. F. Torrance writes this on the matter[8]:

> In the strict sense God alone is Person, complete self-sufficient
> Person, who as such is the creative source of all other personal
> being. He is person-creating, or personalising Person, whereas we
> are all creaturely personalised persons. Hence the Incarnation
> means that all God's relations with us within human being are
> acutely personalised, and that it is through His person-creating
> relations with us that we are unceasingly sustained in our personal
> being day by day. Jesus Christ as the incarnate Son of God,
> therefore is personalising Person, whereas we who draw our being
> from him are personalised persons. From being static, human
> personal being is continuously dependent on and dynamically
> upheld by God's person-creating relations with us. Thus in
> Christian theology we cannot but think of the dynamic personalis-
> ing relation between Christ and a human being as beginning with
> his or her conception. If then we want to think of the human
> embryo as 'potentially person', that must be taken to mean, not
> that the embryo is in process of becoming something else, but
> rather that the embryo continues to become what he or she
> already is in relation to Jesus Christ the incarnate Word of God.

When we speak of the Triune God as 'Personal', we are
speaking of that which is qualitatively different to the persons of
human beings. Christ as the Word of God is Divine Person, but
he personalizes, creates persons, by virtue of the fact he is the
Incarnate Word of God. Our humanity as 'personal' is contingent
to and from his humanity in its union with the Word. It is as this
Incarnate Word that he is THE image of God, for he images that
which he is. We are created IN the Image of God, and in that
short word IN, the whole of our contingency to and from the
Incarnate Word is contained.

Time being inseparably bound with existence, it would seem
that we should regard time in the same way. 'Our time', that is,
our existence, is contingent to and from the time of the Word
made flesh. But the time of the Word made flesh consists in the
relation between the Word as God in his uncreated Time and the
flesh of the Word in its time. It would further seem that this

time of the Word made flesh is not just an episode within history
– it is that – but that episode on which all history depends.

If it be but an episode within history, then there must be a
detachment of history from God in that he enters it only at a
given time. But if the Incarnation of the Word is simultaneous in
the Time of God, to the creative decree of God in bringing all
things into being out of nothing, so that the Incarnation is the
principle of all creation, the Beginning of ways, then all existence
and time is seen to be related to God 'instantly' and is in and
from that two-fold new Beginning for God as Creator and as
Incarnate. All existence and all time, therefore, is seen to be
contained within that Beginning. Hence in the refracted nature
of our time, that is, the created dimension of our existence, we
become what we already are in Christ.

As Christ is both Beginning and End, Alpha and Omega, the
fulfilment of our time, what we will be at the end of our time, is
there also.

This is not a deterministic view, for the principle of contingency operates, so that, created instantly in that Beginning for
God, in his Time, both the dependency we have on God and the
freedom we enjoy to be what we are, is already there in the
creative economy of God. Indeed, contingency from, the freedom
we have in our created identity, can only be safeguarded by this
suggested juxtaposition and corollary of Creation and Incarnation
as the two sides of the one new Beginning for God. For by
creating in Incarnation, he takes to himself the threat which such
freedom poses, and in union with himself contains it within the
grasp of his loving purposes, fulfilling creation, time and existence
in such a way that it remains as freedom but not an ultimately
destructive force leading to chaos and nothingness. He binds, by
creation in Incarnation, the existence and time of all the created
dimension in contingency to and contingency from himself, that
the latter form of contingency may remain but not at the expense
of the other.

In the beginning, in other words, because it is a beginning in
the new Beginning for God, the fulfilment is 'instantly' there, all
time and existence and personage present in the Present of God.
It is instantly recapitulate, and it is this recapitulation which we
experience in our temporal existence as a refraction of the
singularity of its totality.

What we are 'already' there, we live out as the refraction of that in our 'here' and 'now'. That 'here' and 'now', the time and place which is our existence, can be, it may be suggested, understood only by reference to God's Time and Place, what he 'eternally' is, his existence as the Father of the Son and as Son of the Father, both bound in the bond of Divine Love who is the Holy Spirit. In that Time and Place he has made room for and given time to, his creation in its totality, by making for himself a new Beginning in which he 'becomes' Creator, the Word made flesh. It is in that Beginning that creation has its beginning and its fulfilment; its totality as a dynamic present encompassed and held by the Dynamic Present of God. The Word made flesh is that point of reference.

We may think that we live on a flat plane of day succeeding day from birth to death. That is how it appears from our perspective within this created dimension. From God's 'dimension' all time would appear as a ball, held in its totality by him in his uncreated Time. The world is round and not flat! Is this how to view time – that we are already dead and raised in Christ in the fulfilment of our days? We would then look at time, or rather the temporal existence of all creation, as a totality already completed instantly in its inception, and held in love by its Author and Finisher, which is the entrance – the *secret place* of Augustine – into an understanding of it.

> [Christ] is the image of God, the firstborn of every creature; for by him were all things created, that are in heaven and that are in earth, visible and invisible, whether they be thrones, or dominions, or principalities, or powers; all things were created by him and for him: and he is before all things, and by him all things consist.[9]

This, I would suggest, is the key to a unitary understanding of time.

10
Time: an Excursus on the Seventh Day

THUS the heavens and the earth were finished, and all the host of them. And on the seventh day God finished his work which he had done, and he rested on the seventh day from all his work which he had done. So God blessed the seventh day, and hallowed it, because on it God rested from all his work which he had done on creation.[1]

The various hexaemerons written throughout the centuries – Basil (with Gregory of Nyssa's completion), Ambrose, Bede, Grossesteste, Swan – gloss over any significance which they might have found concerning the seventh day's importance in the Genesis myth of creation. When it is mentioned, it is so merely by way of a full stop at the end of a sentence, little more than the satisfactory conclusion of an episode.

Yet the narrator of the myth (or the various editors of it, if one prefers literary to oral criticism or a combination of the two) seems to demand that more attention is paid to the seventh day. Its significance, in dealing with the question of time, seems to be more than only etiological, liturgical or sociological interpretations of it would suggest. It is more than the reading back in story form of a justification of Israel's sabbath observance. In conjunction with the issue of time it has a profound theological dimension to which the narrator (or the editors) perhaps unconsciously point.

Jacques Ellul has an interesting interpretation of the seventh day's significance,[2] though not based on the consideration of the nature of time. He would have it that the 'crown' of creation is not mankind, but this day of God's rest. He cites the *Zohar*, which is the classical text of the *Kabbalah*, or 'Hebrew Tradition', that esoteric Jewish theosophical system with strong roots reaching back to gnosticism. The *Zorah*, or the *Book of Splendour*, was written circa 1280 by the Spanish Jew, Moses de Leon. It states that the sabbath was not created because of the six days; the six days were created for the sabbath. In other words, all that precedes the seventh day finds its fulfilment in the seventh day.

This, says Ellul, points to the fact that when creation was completed with the stamping of His image on creation in the existence of humanity, God has nothing more to do. He retires, he rests, for all has been achieved. This is a rest not of idleness, but of completeness. He stops creating.

What Ellul is trying to do here in a rather surprising way is to underline, first, the claim that God is not a cause, and, second, that humanity is created free.

God is not to be regarded as even the Prime Cause. For a cause cannot cease its functions. It must go on *ad infinitum*. God's rest contradicts such ideas about him. He freely delineates his own sphere of activity so that man may be free in his sphere. If God were a cause, man would not be created free.

It could be said that here Ellul apparently exhibits little appreciation of the principle of double contingency, and the quality and nature of freedom bestowed by that side of contingency which is contingency from God. That freedom is genuine freedom, for it is not, as Ellul seems to suggest, an unrestricted take-it-or-leave-it liberty whereby man would be at the mercy of himself, but, because contingency from is inseparable to contingency to, it is the freedom which man enjoys in strict conformity to the intent of his creation, to be created free for God, and therefore free to be what he really is. The criticism which may arise at this point that the freedom of humanity which Ellul describes is irresponsible freedom, is, however, premature.

Yet, the critic having so embarked could also continue by claiming that Ellul's concept of freedom raises questions as to the relationship between existence and responsibility and freedom. Certainly he distinguishes between the freedom given to man as created and what that has turned into as a result of what he calls *the break with God,* namely independence or autonomy, *a feeble reflection* of genuine freedom. The critic might yield that to this extent Ellul does have a little appreciation of the concept of contingency.

But the criticism might be strengthened by the fact that Ellul still insists that God does not suppress this laissez faire human freedom for he has retired into his rest, leaving all up to human decision. He further goes on to insist that this does not mean that God is indifferent or in absence. For God is a Person and he is

Love and has respect for that which he has created. It is as Personal Love that he exists in relation to us and with us. And he is interested in his creation. The criticism might conclude that this is totally inadequate and renders God an absentee, whatever Ellul may say, or, at the best, portray him as a God impotent to act, whatever interest he might have.

Certainly Ellul's style and blunt assertions lay him open to such adverse reaction. Yet he is pointing to something which has not been taken into consideration by and large.

This underlines the necessity of caution in terminology in trying to describe what lies beyond time. By this I do not mean that Ellul is to be condemned for incaution. Bluntly precipitate he may be, but the caution should come in listening to what is said, and pointed to, in the usage of temporal terms (remembering that that is all any of us has), rather than rushing to criticize, as though someone had been able to contain the whole truth of the matter within the bounds and compass of their thoughts and words.

Criticize certainly, but after due consideration and patient listening; for there is too much precipitate rising in deaf and blind wrath in such matters. This reduces any attempt to come to grips with such issues to but a meaningless squabble within the relativities of our temporal existence, when there may be a genuine attempt to put these relativities in the context of that to which they are all related.

So many theological debates through the centuries have been conducted in this manner, and we are back at an entanglement in three-dimensional absurdities. Indeed, perhaps if what passes for orthodoxy had listened more patiently and charitably to the supposed heretics from time to time, orthodoxy might have realized that the heretics were pointing to judgment on the vacuum which orthodoxy had created by not addressing itself to one issue or another. In so rectifying the matter in a less hastily condemnatory way, it might have saved itself from much of the dullness and deadening legalism which is the tempting refuge to which it sometimes resorts; finding itself on an exciting and adventurous path, beckoned on by the compelling nature of its object of study.

'Let every man be swift to hear, slow to speak, slow to wrath',[3] is perhaps advice to be taken more seriously. It allows in that necessary awe and humility before the incomprehensible and immeasurable God with whom we have to do in his self-revelation. This is particularly true with regard to speaking about the mystery of time. While, after consideration, doctrines such as that of double predestination may be dismissed as inconsistent with the nature of the self-revelation of God, and seen to be an attempt to come to a satisfactory conclusion about that which is essentially mystery by jumping to conclusions via a mistaken syllogistic reasoning, nevertheless the positing of such doctrines should make us aware of the necessity of coming to terms with, for example, the foreknowledge and omnipotence of God, and what these issues mean in exact consistency with the light of that self-revelation.

Ellul's idea of freedom, which is exemplified in his work *The Ethics of Freedom*: (Eerdmans, 1976), seems to be nothing more than the absolute opposite to the concept of double predestination, and worthy of as definite a discarding as its opposite.

But his essentially Christocentric approach[4] to the matter demands that he be heard. God's presence and love, for Ellul, is actualized on earth in Jesus Christ. Christ has dealt with the two things which disturb God's rest – the suffering of human history to which God is not indifferent, and the misunderstanding caused by the sight and experience of such suffering as to the reality of God's love.

In other words, Ellul fixes the reality of the frailty and the wayward freedom of the created dimension, whereby contingency to God is suppressed in the elevation of contingency from God, firmly on the fact of the Word made flesh.

If Ellul is not dismissed perfunctorily, he may be seen to be pointing to a serious consideration of the concept of the seventh day in terms of what he calls *the patience of God*. Here there is implicit a view of time. It is in and under that patience that we live and move and have our being as created beings. We live in the seventh day, for the biblical treatment of this day singles it out in contrast to the other days of creation in the myth. These are described as having an evening and a morning. But not the seventh day; there is no eighth day following. Therefore we live in this 'day' and in the rest of God which characterizes it. The whole of human history takes place in this seventh day, and, indeed, in that history the human agency continues, according to Ellul, the work of creation. This statement might irritate critics even more, as, out of context it suggests that God has capitulated as Creator and thrown the whole burden of that responsibility on to humanity. But it is here that Ellul's essentially Christocentric thought is to be held in mind.

The import of the seventh day is seen primarily for Ellul in the biblical observation that God blessed the seventh day.

Here I wish to go further than Ellul. He sees blessing as implying three constituents; kneeling, pardon and salvation. All human history is included in this blessing even before that history began. That history however is not determined by God, but by human freedom. Providence is so dismissed. If God were behind that history as a cause or director or manipulator, the question has to be asked 'Where do we place the totality of history?' The end of the sixth day is the time of our debut, so it cannot be placed there. Nor can it be so between the end of the sixth and the beginning of the seventh, for the myth categorically assumes the presence of the seventh day (so Ellul; presumably on the basis that there is no mention of the morning of the seventh day).

It is in this seventh day, blessed by God, that all history unfolds by the agency of human freedom. This is Ellul's way of coping with the problem of evil and its relation to the Creator. Here he seems to be entangled in the absurdities and difficulties of temporal thought. He is intent in avoiding any idea of providence, the continual overseeing of creation by its Creator. For if the concept is allowed then, since providence implies that God does everything, he must do that which is evil, for nature and history proceed badly.

But if we shift this argument into the context of instant creation, where all time is a dynamic Now in the Divine and dynamic Present of God, then a different panorama opens out.

The seventh day may then be treated as a mythological way of describing the fulness of creation, and the blessing of God the act and event of the Word made flesh. The Incarnation is the taking stock by God of the frailty and liability of the created dimension to imperfection, as he alone is perfect. The Incarnation is the way taken by God in creating, so that its freedom is assured and its identity as creation established, and the cost of that borne by himself. This rules out the awkwardness of the language of Ellul's thesis in being vulnerable to the accusation that God has withdrawn. It also cancels out his dubious observation that God acts only when this freedom gets out of hand. This latter emphasis does suggest that God is contingent upon the

development of that human freedom in making its own history –
that it is humanity which writes its own epic, God merely
inserting a necessary corrective in Christ's coming.

The idea that the motif of the seventh day is the sphere of
human history under the blessing of God, that is, the compulsion
of the love of the Word made flesh who kneels in humiliation,
receives pardon on behalf of all and establishes the 'salvation'
(that is the right ordering and relation to God) of all creation,
leads to a radical proposition. That is, that we are living out in
our dimension, in the nature of our existence, in the spate of
experiences, circumstances, pains, happinesses, doubts and hopes,
the creative act of God through the Word made flesh. It is
parallel, but more cosmically so, that we are, as Kierkergaard
said[5] with regard to the passion of our Lord, not spectators and
beholders in a past event, but accomplices in a contemporary
event. We live out the act of creation which is but an instant, the
twinkling of an eye as it were, for God in his Present.

A dynamism is thereby given to recapitulation, the gathering
up of all things (and time as a consequence), in Christ. Recapitulation takes on a creative as well as a redemptive significance.

I would also suggest that this puts any discussion on the
nature of time on a different plane. Time is to be viewed as the
totality of existence in its relation to that which gave it existence. Theologically, the quality and nature of that relation is
expressed in terms of the Incarnation, but, I further suggest,
the Incarnation as the mode of the creative act of God in
bringing all things out of nothing and determining their created
dimension.

For too long we have concentrated on the measurement of
time as the nature of time, and fitted the concepts of Creation
and Incarnation (and the issues of our own existences) into this.
That is the anachronism of time.

I am suggesting a Copernican revolution on the matter,
whereby the relativity of time to its source, and the instantly
fulfilled nature of time in that totality, determines our attitude
to, and regard of, time. Principally, of course, this is an exercise
in the relativity of existence to, and its fulfilment as totality in, its
source. Time is to be made secondary to existence; not existence
fitted into time. The two are inseparable, time being the co-
creation of existence. 'Newtonian' views of a framework of an
independent thing called time, into which everything else is

fitted, however plausibly scientific this may be, should be revised radically.

Theologically – and more than theologically – this would enable us to view what we call time from a new vantage point, from where we can see that we are viewing the quality of existence, the time of our being and the being of our time, and perceiving the nature of its tragedies and its achievements in a context which colours them in a new light.

Such an attitude from such a view point has surfaced again and again in theological thought. We may think, by way of example, of that sixteenth/seventeenth century Lutheran Pastor and hymn writer, Philip Nicolai. The circumstances in which he wrote his hymn 'Sleepers Wake!' illustrates his way of thinking as he composed the words. His parish in Westphalia had suffered one of the outbreaks of plague on 1597–8. He had already buried a great number of his parishioners. Standing looking at the surrounding scenes of desolation, and hearing his church clock strike midnight, the significance of all this came to him and caused him to compose that hymn. In it, death becomes resurrection; burial a wedding feast; weeping and lamentation become the rejoicing at the coming of the Bridegroom at the fulfilment of time; his poor, sorry town the heavenly Jerusalem.

The cynic may say that this is desperate hope upon hope, a psycholgical compensation. I would suggest that it is the true perception of existence and time, and the interpretation of the parable which these present to us. Our 'now', this 'present time', is seen in the light of the Word made flesh as to how it 'already' stands in the Now of God.

Epilogue: Time Fulfilled

WE BEGAN with noting the difficulty surrounding our language about time, and the necessity of sifting words such as 'past', 'present', 'future', 'now', 'eternity', 'timelessness', which so often are promiscuously and wantonly used. The discipline of theology requires that all terminology is used paradeigmatically, as a pointer to the object of its study, the nature of which object should determine the way in which any term is used fittingly and turned out of its normal usage for this particular employment. I have suggested that the revelation of God, the fact and event and Person of the Word made flesh, is that Object, and that our words have to be moulded in the crucible of what he is and does, in order to be appropriate words. It is the careful usage of that temporal language which is all we have that we can so construct pointers to that which is more than time as we experience it.

Our language must of necessity be seen as parabolic therefore. That does not mean that there is only a tangential relation between God and ourselves and that language cannot have real content. It does – but it can never contain within its created bounds and limitations the uncreated fulness of God. Its real content is its faithfulness to the way which God takes in revealing himself and in acting towards us and for us in Christ. That Christ, the teller of parables, is Parable himself. The 'when' and 'why' and 'where' of his incarnate life may be stated, the fact of God's reality taking our reality into union with himself; the 'how' of all this, never. He confronts us essentially as mystery, but nevertheless as the Way, the Truth and Life itself.

It is this time of God's revelation, the time he has for us in the event and Person of the Word made flesh, which is the entrance into the question of time. Here God's Time takes created time into union with itself, and the relation between the natures of the two is disclosed. Created time is seen here in the context of that which gives it beginning and end, and its nature is thrown into relief. In other words, time can only be understood (and even then only partially) by reference to that which lies beyond its boundaries. It cannot be understood out of itself, for then we involve ourselves in all the contradictions which its refracted nature, measured by us as 'past', 'present' and 'future', throw at us as three-dimensional absurdities. If time is regarded as an entity in itself, divorced from that which gives it beginning and end, and independent of created existence, then we are involved in three-dimension absurdities which are our futile attempts to understand it as a thing which can be measured by our capacity.

We noted this difficulty to be due, for a great part, to the insubstantiality of time as it appears to us – the fact that the past has gone, the future not yet, and the present but the point when both meet yet do not touch.

The way in which time is related to uncreated Time in the incarnation is that of recapitulation. Here is the focal point of all creation in its mode of union with its Creator to whom it is related in its entirety. It is here that his existence, sufficient in itself as the existence of the Triune God, without any compulsion from within to create or any external pressure (and how could there be anything 'outside' God?), declares that his creation is in contingent relation to and from himself. The incarnation demonstrates that creation is a matter of the sheer love and grace of God, gathering and touching all created existence, and therefore all time, so that it is both dependent upon him for its existence yet has its own existence as qualitatively different from the existence of God. He gives it, and sustains it, in its freedom and the freedom of its own identity and dimension – its contingency from – which can only be true freedom, and not utter, destructive chaos, in that it reposes in that beginning and sustaining – its contingency to him.

The Incarnation, the fact and event and Person of the Word made flesh, means that recapitulation is the concentration and declaration of double contingency, in which the course of created time, its end joined to its beginning, is seen in the illumination of uncreated Light in the midst of the created realities, making them his own, and thereby radiating the fulness of years.

It is here that theology, as a discipline in its own right, has to begin, and return in constant reference to this beginning, in its efforts to grapple with the questions which face it. Theology is a Christocentric exercise. If it is anything else it can be only based on the shifting sand of diverse deductions, which it uses as its authority and justification, picked haphazardly from the created

dimension. Any one such deduction is, in the last resort, as good
as any other, for, since all are from within that dimension, one is
as authoritative or otherwise as the other.

The place of humanity in creation is of import to a theological
understanding of the nature of creation. The act of creation is
bounded by the bringing into being of two rational factors – light
as the first form of created matter and human existence. These
typify creation as a creation of rationality. It is a creation of light
and therefore of created illumination and reason, perceived and
regarded and described as such by the rational stature of human
being informed by it. Man is given a vocation and estate within
and towards creation on God's behalf. He is made in the image
of God, and as such fulfils that existence and role, to guard, tend
and explore the order which God has bestowed on creation. He is
given a responsibility in light towards God on behalf of creation.

Both light and humanity are fundamentally related to the
Creator, the Word of God by whom all things were made, for
whom all things were made, and in whom all things consist. He
is, as the Son, one with the Father in the bond of Divine Love
the Holy Spirit, uncreated Light, Light of Light, Very God of
Very God, eternally begotten, not made. And he is the Word
made flesh, bone of our bone, flesh of our flesh, blood of our
blood, assuming into union with himself all that we are, the full
constituency of human being. As God made man, he illuminates
humanity, enlightens it. As man in union with God he offers to
God the perfect response of humanity enlightened on behalf of
all.

The Word made flesh, Jesus Christ, came to minister the
things of God to man and the things of man to God. He is both
the Author of the loving reason for our existence and our
response of fulfilment of – our 'amen' to – the bestowal of that
existence. He brings the whole of creation to bear on his Divine
existence, the source of its illumination and rationality, its beginning and its end. The incarnation is a cosmic and total event and
accomplishment.

But the question of the relation of the Word as uncreated
Time and Light to created time and light, unfolds. Are the act of
creation and the fact of the incarnation two 'events' in the
working of God, separated by time? Various figures throughout
the history of Christian thought seem to point to the dilemma of
that conclusion (Irenaeus tentatively, Grosseteste more strongly,

for example). If creation and Incarnation are so separated by time, as acts as they are in themselves, that is, acts of God, then God is contingent to created time and the whole existence of creation. The conclusion can only be drawn surely that God created, creation moved outside the grasp of God, and God had to act after a lapse of time.

But such a conclusion is jumped to only because of the syllogistic reasoning of three-dimensional thought which omits the all important middle necessary in a syllogism. That middle is that uncreated Time, the Time of God, and created time, 'our' time, are qualitatively different. It is a conclusion arrived at through the absurdity of three-dimensional calculation and measurement, and applying that to the existence of God. This is not to say that Goes does not have anything to do, and cannot have anything to do, with the reality of creation as temporal existence. It is to claim that we must not think that God sees and acts towards time and creation on the basis of a mere historical event, and that the whole significance of his looking and acting can be circumscribed by temporal points on the assumption that time moves on a straight line.

This has been compounded by philosophical questions concerning infinity. We need only look at Richard Sorabji's analysis of the problems of infinity and creation's possible beginning, as exemplified by the efforts of the later Neo-Platonists against Aristotelian definitions, and the contribution of John Philoponos in the sixth century from the Christian standpoint of philosophical discussion, to realize the constantly revolving, never resolving, meanderings on the subject, which Sorabji so masterfully outlines.[1]

There is a morass of tangled thoughts in the competitive claims of Aristotle[2] that infinity always has something outside it, because

> For in general infinity exists through one thing always being taken for another, what is taken being always finite, but ever other and other.

Infinity for Aristotle, is, as Sorabji perceives (and to use his phrase) an *extendible finitude*. It is not all-encompassing. This has an echo in the contemporary idea of gradually coming closer to a limit – that is, the half of one plus the quarter plus the eighth plus the sixteenth and so on infinitely, does just this with the limit one. It never achieves that limit but moves towards it infinitely by adding finite portions. This approach is further made complex by questions as to whether an infinite line is made up of actual or potential divisions, (Aristotle claimed only potentiality for it), or if infinity has within itself infinite parts (whole numbers, for example, are said to contain an infinite set of odd numbers or an infinite set of even numbers), and such questions so on ad infinitum.

Philoponos pointed out[3] that the universe must have a beginning, otherwise it would have gone through, already, an infinity of years. That being the case, then next year would be infinity plus one, which is ridiculous. But is there a hint here that what we call 'infinity' must in fact be an instant, all-embracing episode?

Instead of indulging in the particular cut and thrust concerning infinity, I prefer Grosseteste's view that all our vaunted infinities are finite to God, and are, in any case, more a comment on the limitations of the human mind than objective projections. (It may be added here that Grosseteste's similarity of thought to Philoponos may well be because Philoponos's thought was known to some Arabic writers and commentators, and with some of these works Grosseteste was familiar and by them partially influenced, Averroes in particular).

Indeed, in both Neo-Platonic and Aristotelian systems, little is said about the limitations of the thinker's mind projecting the particular theories (though much is said about their opponents' shortcomings). Grosseteste is the most honest in the matter with his perpetual disclaimers of ability in such matters.

That the universe has a beginning is orthodox Christian theology. We looked at the way in which this was emphasised by Basil in his *Hexaemeron*, and how this was taken up by Grosseteste. What was then emphasised was the role of light in creation, and Grosseteste's observation that it was the first form of created matter in the beginning, which instantly at its creation expanded, as only light can, equally in all directions, inseparable to matter, as form must be, and thus determining the shape and quality and nature of the universe, as what to us is an infinite sphere, and radiating illumination (*lumen* rather than *lux* which Grosseteste uses for first light and its activity) back to its centre, again instantly.

The place and priority and determining role of light suggests in Grosseteste's thought that all creation is instant. The six days of creation are interpreted as simultaneous cycles in the angelic intelligences, angels being the first and purest creatures of created light.

We went on to suggest that this a recapitulation in reverse, as it were. We live in the created dimension which has time as its co-creation, as a function of its existence. This dimension may be regarded as the refraction of a single beam of light, the refraction from our side being the aeons, centuries, decades, years and days of creation's existence, while it is all but one single beam from God's side.

This brought into consideration the relation of this instant beginning to the fact that God 'becomes' what he was not 'before' (to apply, out of the necessity of having nothing else, temporal concepts, but emptied of their temporal content and application, to God) – namely he 'becomes' Creator. This is a new Beginning for God, and it is in contingency to and from that new Divine Beginning that the beginning of creation is related.

God 'becomes' Creator, not just part Creator, or beginning to evolve as Creator, but completely Creator, in that new Beginning. So too, creation is in its entirety, its beginning and its end, there at its beginning.

The alternative to this, it was suggested, was that God is contingent upon time, and is to be seen as endless time. But that reduces him to nothing more than qualitatively the same as time and therefore as creation. He is but time and creation writ large, being on the same dimension. On this ground of thought, it is difficult to see how time and therefore things have a beginning, and we end up with a variant on the 'eternity' of the world.

A further consideration of the relation between God and creation, God and time, centres on the relation of creation to incarnation. Does God create and creation grow out with his control, so that he has to act to rectify matters, and does so in the incarnation? This separates the moment of creation and the moment of the incarnation. Certainly this appears to be the case from our side in the created dimension of time.

But what does this say about God's omniscience and omnipotence? Not to mention his ability? His omnipotence and omniscience are not to be looked at as if they were human power and knowing to the nth degree.

But if, as Christian theology claims, his power and knowledge are the way of Jesus Christ, the Word made flesh, is not the very act of creation accomplished in Incarnation simultaneously and instantly from the side of God? Otherwise, if there is a time lapse, we have projected temporal measurement into God and still his competence is questionable.

The way of creation, is, it may be suggested, the way of the Word made flesh. The cost to God in creating an entity other than himself with its own dimension and identity is his self-involvement in the danger and threat of nothingness to that creation, which, 'less' and other than himself, must have an existence constantly threatened by non-being. This self-involvement is the Incarnation of the Son or Word by whom all things were made.

The suggestion in full is that in that Beginning for God, which he takes upon himself in sheer overflowing love and in grace, Christ is the Beginning and the End, the Alpha and the Omega, joining the beginning of creation to its end instantly. But this is in that 'eternal' dimension of God which embraces all time and things instantly.

What is called 'eternity', with its popular confusion with 'endless time', is better described as God's Time, qualitatively and incomprehensible different from our time in this created dimension.

Only by reference to that instant in the Time of God, where all time and things are contemporaneous, which we experience as refracted time, can the question of time be addressed.

Created time, or rather, more strictly speaking, time co-created as an expression and function of created things, may be regarded as contingent to and from the Time of God, or rather, again, more strictly speaking, to and from the God whose Divine existence is his Time.

The Time of God is the existence and Place of God; created time is our existence and place. Time is not a separate, independent entity. That is the mistake we make in thinking about it, and that leads us into all the theological debates concerning universalism, double predestination, and so on, which are born of the absurdities of three-dimensional thinking in isolation from the dimension of God's Time.

It is this dimension of God's Time, concentrated on the Word made flesh, the Invisible made visible, the Incomprehensible comprehensible, wherein our time is in contingent union with that Time of God, to which we should constantly refer in all our thinking about time. That is a matter of thinking in terms of quality and not quantity. Unfortunately the latter is our besetting sin in thinking about time which we confuse with our measurement of it in the created dimension.

What then of the end of time, its fulfilment?

Our existence and therefore what we call our time, moves from its beginning to its end. It is not otherwise. This is time's direction, or, more properly in view of what has been stated about the relation of time and existence, the direction of life. In the dimension of created time, or rather again, time co-created with the substance of creation, there was a time when we were not. We were not yet born into this one directional flow of created being. It is perhaps surprising that the question of our end occupies our thoughts much more than the question of our beginning. Yet the perplexity is of the same nature. 'What were we before birth?' is as enigmatic as 'What will we be when we die?' *Whence I come I know not, I go and know not whither.* This is the question of non-being, which in turn is the question of the boundary of this movement into and out of life.

To take time as an independent entity, as something to be measured into past, present and future, and to see our existence in that light, will forcibly remind us of non-being. We have touched already on the futility of such a view of time and the dubiety of any certainty of such measurement, the past having gone, the future not yet, and the present so infinitesimal that it defies quantifying. The reality of our existence, if it is regarded according to this sort of measurement of time, is in question! Is anything in our life, even that life itself, tangible and stable?

Again we have suggested already that a consideration of time, that is, created existence, is recapitulate in its entirety as a dynamic present in the Dynamic Present of God's uncreated existence. Its beginning is within and distinct from that new Beginning for God whereby he 'becomes' Creator as well as Father. This new Beginning is the act of creation and incarnation in that Present of God, whereby all things are created and held in their contingent integrity by the Word made flesh.

It is suggested further that this present in which all creation and all time therefore is 'instant' before God, is what we experience as refracted existence and time. It is in the creation of the singularity of light, by the One who is uncreated Light, that all light is contained. Creation is a creation of light and it is held in contingency to and by that uncreated Light by whose grace the darkness of non-being does not engulf it. The question of non-being does not therefore arise. That is a question which has been tackled and answered by God alone in the fact of the Word made flesh. It is not one for us to seek to solve, for its solution is already there in Jesus Christ. That is the Light which has shone in the darkness and dispelled the threat of non-being and the onrush of complete chaos, and that is the Light which lights every one who comes into the world.

We therefore come from God, not in the sense that we are an extension or an emanation of God, but from that fulness of existence and time in which his decree is instantaneously actualized in the creative act through the Word made flesh who holds that fulness in contingent relation to himself. And we therefore go to God. When time ends for us, that is, when our existence reaches its conclusion in this dimension in which we live and move and have our being, that fulness is what remains. It is not that we shall be as those who have been, that we have passed into the negation of being. Rather, it is the gathering up of our whole life into what it 'already' is as a dynamic present in the Present of God's existence. The refracted rays of what we were in our days pass back into the single beam of light in which they were present at the beginning of creation which includes its end in that act of instantaneous creation.

The whole sweep of time from the beginning to the end, the total existence of creation, is lived out in what we measure as days and years, but it is the living out of that which is 'instantly' present to God in his Present.

This defies all attempts at measurement by any means we know. For it concerns not quantity by quality. Again and again the whole question is obscured by the insistent attempt by man to quantify, to see the significance of time by its length and that length relative to a supposed infinity which is called 'eternity' or (absurdly) 'timelessness'. It was this problem which Grosseteste saw when he pointed out that even our infinities are finite to God. Any view of time must begin with the awareness that the problem of time cannot be solved, or even entered, by such measurement.

The measurement with which we ought to be concerned is that of quality, and that brings us into the realm of existence and its nature. Time is not, it must be repeated, an entity in itself, independent and quantifiable as an isolated creature. What we call 'time' is, in the last resort, a human convenience, a means of regulating the movement or rest of our being, of giving our existence a framework of expedient order. But we tend to elevate that order out of the realm of the secondary and make it primary and determinative. *Time is money* is one of the attitudes thrown up by such a process. This may well be true for that which sees its being as governed by time and time as that which is opposed to existence as an implacable foe. But it can say nothing to the quality of existence in its proper οἰκονομία – its authentic order – as a created reality contingent to and from God in his Word. The parables concerning riches may well be interpreted in this light. The only measurement of quality we can have is hinted at in the biblical imagery of such phrases as that of our creation *in the image of God,*[4] of *the measure of the stature of the fulness of Christ,*[5] and all that points to what Athanasius called *a life in correspondence to God* to which we are called in our creation.

Time should be regarded in the light of the experience of existence, not in the subjective way of Augustine, but by referring that experience, be it happiness or sorrow, tears or laughter, loneliness or companionship, to its recapitulation and its resolution in the Word made flesh.

It is on the basis of those 'mathematics' that St Paul *reckons the sufferings of this present time not worthy to be compared to the glory that shall be revealed.*[6] When the doctrine of recapitulation in Christ, when Incarnation is juxtaposed in the Present of God's Time with the act of creation, there is the sum of such reckoning. The bringing of creation into being out of non-being and the constant threat of that non-being to creation, is the dilemma which God enters in his loving purpose of creation. The dilemma is entered at Incarnation, chaos is contained by crucifixion, order is affirmed in resurrection. That is the cost borne by God in creating, and it is a cost which bears the giving of freedom to an entity other than himself, to be itself and yet to be his. In that bearing the beginning is joined to the end, the inception is the fulfilment, and all temporal existence is a dynamic present in the Present of God in his Word. Our temporal existence is the refraction of that single recapitulation in which we become what we are 'already' in our created freedom and order bestowed by God in creating in this way. It can only be understood, and even then only partially, by reference to that on which and from which it is contingent existence. It is to be understood in its totality as it rests as a dynamic present in the Present of God in his incarnate Word. This is the ground for the optimistic estimation of our temporal existence, the span of our days, the epic of mankind and the aeons of creation.

> I saw Eternity the other night
> Like a great Ring of pure and endless light,
>   All calm, as it was bright;
> And round beneath it, Time, in hours, days, years,
>   Driven by the spheres
> Like a vast shadow moved, in which the world
> And all her train were hurled.[7]

Statements abound throughout this book. But they are not meant to be conclusions. Indulgence is requested for them, for they have been made under the double priviso of the awareness of the impropriety of all language when it is directed to that which is beyond this created dimension in which we live and move and have our being – and think and talk and write – and of acquiesence to St Paul's observation – even the 'dogmatic' Paul – that we know but in part.

No conclusions are drawn in this book in fact. What statements have been made are to be construed as but goads to further thoughts which others may feel prodded to take up, positively or negatively, by agreement or dispute, as they will – provided their thoughts are, as mine have attempted to be, constructed as pointers towards the incomprehensible and measureless God, who is, within our limitations of this created world, comprehensible as the span of a child in a manger.

Even if all that has been written on the previous pages had been dictated by the tongues of angels, there still would be no conclusions. I am aware that what I have written will pass as sounding brass or tinkling cymbals into that which is gone, but, hopefully, it will echo a few chords in others' awareness. For this has been written primarily in awareness of that charity of God in the act of creation and towards his creation, which can but evoke an amen of love towards God and his handiwork from all of us.

Perhaps there is a pointer to the truth in Irenaeus's claim that man was created as a child. Before the perplexity of our temporal existence, the problem of time, we stand at all times like children. We may think that we have become the man and put away childish things, and have a mature perception. We may think that we have put away the childish perception of a two dimensional drawing, with a flat sky over a flat earth peopled with matchstick figures, and have come to the ability to draw out and colour in a three-dimensional scene. So we fabricate with cunning and skill, when we become the man, the portrayal of our temporal existence. And that too is but a delusion, for the canvas on which either child or man paints is still flat.

Before the mystery of time, the question of our existence, our intellect is but limited.

In looking at the works of those authors throughout the centuries whom I have cited in these pages, there would appear to be one constant factor which may point to a conclusion. They all knew that they saw through a glass darkly and piecemeal.

We may recall the Psalmist struck dumb before God, of Job placing his hand to cover his mouth when God answers him, of Augustine laying down his restless pen of determinism and autobiography in the knowledge of final rest in God, of Athanasius's awareness that he was at that place in talking about the things of God where the cherubim and seraphim veil their faces and spread the covering of their wings, of Barth capitulating his myriad of words in confession before the overwhelming grace of God.

They all knew that only when we are brought and stand as contemporaries before God, will we see face to face. That, I would suggest, is the reality of the totality of time in its dynamic present in which what we are in all our days is gathered up in the fulfilment of all creation where it abides in the Present of the God who in love has created all things by the grace of his Word.

We may think that the mountains before us in our created dimension may be scaled by our self-endeavours, conquered and removed. But over and beyond them all, Mount Zion, the dwelling place of God in Light uncreated, towers before us as that which is unconquerable by our supposed self-sufficiency and vaunted wits. Yet it is by and in the illumination of love of the light of that Place where all things are fulfilled that we may climb up or remove our own particular mountains, and, having done that, see, as we have never seen before, the Way thereto.

Our life and death, our time and what we are in our time, are affirmed by their fulfilment in the Time of God. It is the permission for our individual participation in that instant creative

act, which is God's alone, which has cost him dearly as the Word
made flesh, and which is the love of God in creating an entity
other than himself whose end is to enjoy him and glorify him
forever. *Do you see yonder shining light?* Pilgrim is asked.[8] *I think
so*, he answers – and on he goes.

> Lord, thou hast been our refuge: from one generation to another.
>
> Before the mountains were brought forth, or ever the earth and
> the world were made: Thou art God from everlasting, and world
> without end.
>
> Thou turnest man to destruction: again thou sayest, Come
> again, ye children of men.
>
> For a thousand years in thy sight are but as yesterday: seeing
> that is past as a watch in the night.
>
> As soon as thou scatterest them they are even as a sleep: and
> fade away suddenly like the grass.
>
> In the morning it is green and groweth up: but in the evening
> it is cut down, dried up, and withered.
>
> For we consume away in thy displeasure: and are afraid at thy
> wrathful indignation.
>
> Thou has set our misdeeds before thee: and our secret sins in
> the light of thy countenance.
>
> For when thou art angry all our days are gone: we bring our
> years to an end, as it were a tale that is told.
>
> The days of our age are three score years and ten; and though
> men be so strong that they come to four score years: yet is their
> strength then but labour and sorrow; so soon passeth it away and
> we are gone.
>
> But who regardeth the power of thy wrath: for even thereafter
> as a man feareth, so is thy displeasure.
>
> So teach us to number our days: that we may apply our hearts
> unto wisdom.
>
> Turn thee again, O Lord, at the last: and be gracious unto they
> servants.
>
> O satisfy us with thy mercy, and that soon: so shall we be glad
> and rejoice all the days of our life.
>
> Comfort us again now after the time that thou has plagued us:
> and for the years wherein we have suffered adversity.
>
> Shew thy servants thy work: and their children thy glory.
>
> And the glorious majesty of the Lord our God be upon us:
> prosper thou the work of our hands upon us, O prosper thou our
> handy-work.[9]

Notes

Prologue

1. Coveney and Highfield: *The Arrow of Time*, pp. 23ff.
2. A. Eddington: *The Nature of the Physical World*, C.U.P. 1928, p. 91.
3. c.f. Acts 5:38–39.
4. Thomas Traherne: *Select Meditations* (unpublished) cited in *Landscapes of Glory*, ed. A. M. Allchin, p. 21.
5. E.g. Hymn 559 in the *Revised Church Hymnary* (Church of Scotland).
6. Psalm 36:9.
7. Psalm 31:15.
8. Psalm 90:12.
9. Psalm 39:4.
10. Psalm 39:7.
11. Lancelot Andrewes: *Sermon 10 of the Nativitie*, 1635 ed., pp. 86–88.
12. J. W. Dunne: *An Experiment with Time*; Faber and Faber, 1942 (4th ed.), c.f. pp. 132–196.
13. Coveney and Highfield: *The Arrow of Time*, p. 32.

Chapter 1: Theological Questions about Time

1. Karl Barth: *Church Dogmatics*, Vol. 1:2, p. 45. T. and T. Clark, Edinburgh.
2. Athanasius: *Contra Arianos*, 1:20; *Ad Serapionem*, I:2:5, I:9:24.
3. E.g. Irenaeus: *Adversus Haereses*, IV:11:1–5.
4. E.g. Athanasius: *Ad Serapionem*, I:17.
5. Karl Barth: *Church Dogmatics*, Vol.II:1.
6. Karl Barth: *Church Dogmatics*, Vol. I:2, pp. 46ff.
7. Augustine: *Confessions* XI:28.
8. Barth: *Commentary on the Epistle to the Romans*, pp. 29, 30. O.U.P.

Chapter 2: Recapitulation and Time

1. Irenaeus: *Demonstration of the Apostolic Preaching*, 3.
2. Irenaeus: *Adversus Haereses* III:10:2, IV:14:2, V:1:1, V:27.
3. Irenaeus: *Demonstration of the Apostolic Preaching*, 3.
4. Athansius: *Ad Serapionem* I:16, c.f. Gregory Nazianzen: *Orations* XXXI:7.
5. c.f. Irenaeus,: *Adversus Haereses* I:30:1.
6. E.g. Irenaeus: *Adversus Haereses*, II:13:3–4, 8, 10, Athanasius: *In Illud Omnia*, 3–5; *De Decretis*, 12: *Contra Arianos*, I:20, II:30, III:3,10, *Ad Serapionem*, I:19f.
7. Deuteronomy 28:37.
8. Jeremiah 24:9.
9. Gregory Nazianzen: *Orations*, XXVIII:9 – c.f. Athanasius: *Ad Mon*, 2, Basil: *Con. Eun.* I:10.
10. c.f. Irenaeus: *Adversus Haereses*, I:15:4, III:16:6, 19:1–3.
11. Irenaeus: *Demonstration of the Apostolic Preaching*, 11.
12. Irenaeus: *Adversus Haereses*, III:21:10, IV:pref. 3, IV:19:2, 20:1,4, 39:2–3, V:1:2–3, 5:1, 6:1, 15:2, 16:1, 28:4.
13. Irenaeus: *Demonstration of the Apostolic Preaching*, 11.
14. *Apostolic Constitutions*: VIII:12.
15. Irenaeus: *Demonstration of the Apostolic Preaching*, 12 c.f. *Ad. Haer*, II:30:7, V:5:1.
16. Irenaeus: *Demonstration of the Apostolic Preaching*, 12.

17. E.g. Irenaeus: *Adversus Haereses* III:18:7, 21:10, IV:36:4, V:1:1–2, 15:3. *Demonstration of the Apostolic Preaching*, 31, 34.

18. E.g. Irenaeus: *Adversus Haereses* III:22:4, *Demonstration of the Apostolic Preaching*, 33.

19. E.g. 1, Irenaeus: *Adversus Haereses* II:25:3, III:16:6, 17:1, 18:7, 19:3,6–8, 20:2, 22:3, IV:33:11, V:2:1, 15:1, 16:1–2, *Demonstration of the Apostolic Preaching*, 30ff.

20. Hippolytus: *Against Beron and Helix*, Frag.II.

21. E.g. Irenaeus: *Adversus Haereses* IV:20:5, 33:4, 34:4.

22. Tertullian: *On Monogamy* V.

23. Jerome: *Against Jovianus*: I:18.

Chapter 3: Creation, Incarnation and Light

1. R. Southern: *Robert Grosseteste – The Growth of an English Mind in Medieval Europe*, p. 195.

2. Grosseteste: *De Cessatione Legalium*, III:ii:1, trans. Southern, op. cit. p. 223.

3. Irenaeus: *Demonstration of the Apostolic Preaching*, 12.

4. Irenaeus: *Demonstration*, 12.

5. Grosseteste: *De Cessatione Legalium*, I:viii:7–13, part of which trans. Southern, op. cit. p. 224.

6. E.g. *Liber Scintillarum: The Book of Shining Lights*.

7. Grosseteste: *Hexaemeron*, I:viii:4 (Dales and Gieben, pp. 60–61).

8. Grosseteste: *Hexaemeron*: VIII:iv:7 (Dales and Gieben, p. 222).

9. James McEvoy: *The Philosophy of Robert Grosseteste*, Clarendon, 1986.

10. R. Southern: *Robert Grosseteste: The Growth of an English Mind in Medieval Europe, p. 219*.

11. *Hexaemeron*: II:X:4, Dales and Gieben, p. 100.

12. *Grosseteste: Commentaries in VIII Libros Physicorum Aristotelis.*

13. Augustine: *De Civitate Dei* XII:18.

14. St Matthew 10:30.

15. Psalm 147:5.

16. Grosseteste: *Hexaemeron*: Book I:I:1, Dales and Gieben, p. 49.

17. Gregory of Nazianzen: *Orationes* XXVIII:9.

18. Hilary of Poitiers: *De Trinitate*, I:19.

19. Gregory of Nyssa: *Against Eunomius*: I:26.

20. Grosseteste: *Hexaemeron*, VIII:1:2.

21. Ambrose: *On the Christian Faith*, I:58,74. But c.f. Athanasius extensively against the Arians.

22. Gregory of Nyssa: *Against Eunomius*: I:26.

23. Basil: *Hexaemeron*, Homily II:7, Homily III:2.

24. Athanasius: *Discourses against the Arians*, I:3:57.

25. *Bodley MS 198*, f.130d: Gregory: *Moralia*, V:34.

26. *Lyons MS 414*, f.23v.

27. Grosseteste: *Hexaemeron*, VIII:1 – XII:2.

28. c.f. Irenaeus: *Adversus Haereses* V:16:2.

29. Irenaeus: c.f. *Adversus Haereses* IV:20:5, IV:33:4, IV:34:4.

30. Southern: *Robert Grosseteste*: p. 222.

31. E.g. Athanasius: *Discourse II against the Arians*, 18–43, 48, *Expositio Fidei*, 4.

32. Justin Martyr: *Dialogue with Trypho*, CXXIX.

33. Justin Martyr: *Dialogue with Trypho*, LXI.

34. Irenaeus: *Adversus Haereses* IV:XX:1–4; c.f., e.g. IV:XXXIV:4.

35. Irenaeus: *Adversus Haereses* IV:XIX:1–3.

36. Irenaeus: *Adversus Haereses* IV:XX:7.

37. Irenaeus: *Adversus Haereses* III:XVI:6.

38. Irenaeus: *Adversus Haereses* III:XI:5.

39. Irenaeus: *Adversus Haereses* I:XXVIII:1, III:XXIII:8.

40. E.g. Irenaeus: *Adversus Haereses* III:18:7, 21:10; IV:36:4; V:1:1–2, 15:3; *Demonstration of the Apostolic Preaching*, 31.

41. Irenaeus: *Demonstration of the Apostolic Preaching*, 11.
42. Irenaeus: *Adversus Haereses* II:1:4.
43. Irenaeus: *Adversus Haereses* II:3:2; c.f. I:12:2.
44. Irenaeus: *Adversus Haereses* II:28:4–5.
45. Irenaeus: *Adversus Haereses* II:13:8.

Chapter 4: Time and Light: the Beginning

1. Irenaeus: *Adversus Haereses* II:13:8. C.f.II:28:4–6.
2. Irenaeus: *Adversus Haereses* II:28:3.
3. Athanasius: *Contra Arianos* II:2.
4. Grosseteste: *Hexaemeron* I:VIII:1–1:X:10.
5. Grosseteste: *Hexaemeron* I:X:10.
6. See above, pp. 14f.
7. Colossians 1:15.
8. Colossians 1:15.
9. Athanasius: *De Incarnatione Verbi Dei* 3–5.
10. Augustine: *Ep.* 187.11.
11. Grosseteste: *Sacerdotes tui induantur iustitiam*: Charge delivered to the clergy on the imitation of angelic contemplation and action, possibly when he was Archdeacon of Leicester.
12. Grosseteste: *Hexaemeron* II:VIII:1ff.
13. Grosseteste: *Dicta*, 29 (translated by R. Southern from a fragment of the text in MSS Bodl, 830 f27).
14. Grosseteste: *Hexaemeron* II:IV–IX, Dale and Gieben, pp. 88–97.
15. C.f. Augustine: *De Civitate Dei* XI:6–9.
16. Augustine: *De Civitate Dei* XI:9.
17. Augustine: *De Civitate Dei* XI:6.
18. Grosseteste: *Hexaemeron* II:vii;1, Dales and Gieben, pp. 94–95.
19. Grosseteste: *Hexaemeron* II:vii:1, Dales and Gieben p. 94.
20. Grosseteste: *Hexaemeron* II:vii:1, Dales and Gieben, p. 95.
21. Grosseteste: *Hexaemeron* II:ii:1: Dales and Gieben, p. 86.
22. Athanasius: *Contra Arianos* I:29.
23. Athanasius: *Contra Arianos* II:2.
24. Gregory Nazianzen: *Orationes* XXXVIII:7, XLV:3.

Chapter 5: The Individual and Time

1. pp. 21ff, 26ff.
2. Coveney and Highfield: *The Arrow of Time*, p. 23.
3. See above, pp. 16f.
4. Job, 38:1ff.
5. C.f. Job 7:6.
6. C.f. Job 14:2.
7. C.f. Job 9:6.
8. C.f. Psalm 39:5.
9. C.f. Psalm 37:1,7.
10. C.f. Psalm 37:16, I Timothy 6:6–9.
11. C.f. Philippians 4:11.
12. C.f. Psalm 5.
13. C.f. Psalm 31:15.
14. Augustine: *Confessions*, I:1.
15. C.f. Philippians 4:11.
16. C.f. II Chronicles 20:7, Isaiah 41:8, James 2:23, Exodus 33:11.
17. C.f. 1 Corinthians 4:6.
18. C.f. 1 Corinthians 12:6.
19. Psalm 139:14–16.
20. E.g. c.f. Colossians 1–3.
21. Gregory of Nyssa: *Against Eunomius I:26*.

22. Gregory of Nyssa: *On the Making of Man* XVI:7ff.
23. Swan: *Speculum Mundi* (including the *Hexameron*), 1642 edition, p. 39.

Chapter 6: Predestination, Universalism and Time

1. Lancelot Andrewes: *Sermon 15 of the Resurrection*, Sermons 1635 edition, p. 548.
2. Lancelot Andrewes: *Sermon preached at St Maries Hospital*, Sermons 1635 edition, p. b81.
3. Laud: *Relation of the Conference*, 1639 edition, the 14th page (un-numbered).
4. Augustine: *Enchiridion* I:5.
5. John Calvin: *De Aeterna Praedestinatione Dei* VIII:4.
6. John Calvin: *De Aeterna Praedestinatione Dei* VIII:6.
7. John Calvin: *De Aeterna Praedestinatione Dei* IV.
8. John Calvin: *De Aeterna Praedestinatione Dei* IV.
9. John Calvin: *De Aeterna Praedestinatione Dei* IV.
10. John Calvin: *De Aeterna Praedestinatione Dei* IV.
11. T. F. Torrance: *The Trinitarian Faith*, p. 88.
12. Colossians 1:17–20.
13. Jacques Ellul: *What I believe*, pp. 188–213.
14. Jacques Ellul: *What I believe*, pp. 191–192.
15. Romans 8:18–25.

Chapter 7: Time Created and Uncreated Time

1. Karl Barth: *Church Dogmatics*, vol. III:2, pp. 437–438.
2. John Swan: *Speculum Mundi* (including the *Hexameron*), 1642 edition, p. 35 – c.f. p. 103 above.
3. Karl Barth: *Church Dogmatics*, vol. III:2, p. 438.
4. Karl Barth: *Church Dogmatics*, vol. I:2, p. 45 – c.f. pp. 17ff above.
5. Dorothy Sayers: *The Nine Tailors*, p. 71, NEL ed, 1977.
6. Karl Barth: *Church Dogmatics*, vol. III:2, pp. 437ff.
7. Karl Barth: *Church Dogmatics*, vol. III:2, p. 459.
8. Karl Barth: *Church Dogmatics*, vol. III:2, p. 460.
9. Karl Barth: *Chuch Dogmatics*, vol. III:2, p. 462.
10. Karl Barth: *Church Dogmatics*, vol. III:2, p. 501.

Chapter 8: Time and its Measurement

1. Lancelot Andrewes: *Sermon I of the Gun-Powder-Treason*; 1635 edition, p. 891.
2. St Augustine: *Confessions*, Book XI:1
3. St Augustine: *Confessions*, Book XI:2.
4. St Augustine: *Confessions*, Book XI:3.
5. St Augustine: *Confessions*, Book XI:8.
6. St Augustine: *Confessions*, Book XI:9
7. See above, p. 85.
8. St Augustine: *Confessions*, Book XI:11.
9. St Augustine: *Confessions*, Book XI:12 – c.f. *De Civitate Dei* XI:4–8.
10. St Augustine: *Confessions*, Book VIII:13.
11. St Augustine: *Confessions*, Book XI:16.
12. St Augustine: *Confessions*, Book XI:17.
13. St Augustine: *Confessions*, Book XI:20.
14. St Augustine: *Confessions*, Book XI:21.
15. St Augustine: *Confessions*, Book XI:22.
16. St Augustine: *Confessions*, Book XI:23.
17. St Augustine: *Confessions*, Book XI:24–26.
18. St. Augustine: *Confessions*, Book XI:26,37.
19. Coveney and Highfield: *The Arrow of Time*, p. 24.

Chapter 9: Time, Place, and Existance

1. St Augustine: *Confessions*, Book XI:22.

2. Stephen Hawking: *A Brief History of Time*, Bantam Press, 1991, pp. 181–182.
3. See above, p. 17.
4. See above, pp. 126ff.
5. Robert Browning: *Pippa Passes.*
6. I Corinthians 15:8.
7. Acts I: 9.
8. T. F. Torrance: *Test Tube Babies: Morals – Science – And the Law*, Scottish Academic Press, 1984, p. 11.
9. Colossians 1:15–17.

Chapter 10: Time: an Excursus on the Seventh Day

1. Genesis 2:1–3.
2. Jacques Ellul: *What I believe*, pp. 152ff.
3. James 1:19.
4. Jacques Ellul: *What I believe*, pp. 161ff.
5. Søren Kierkegaard: *Christian Discourses: Discourses at the Communion on Fridays*, 1848, trans. W. Lowrie, Oxford University Press, 1961, pp. 284, 285.

Epilogue: Time Fulfilled

1. R. Sorabji: *Matter, Space and Motion: Theories in antiquity and their sequel*, Duckworth, 1988, pp. 164ff.
2. Aristotle: *Physica* 3:5, 206a 27–9; 3:6, 206b33ff.
3. John Philoponos: *De Aeternitate Mundi contra Proclum*, ed. Rabe, pp. 9–11, 619.
4. Genesis 1:27.
5. Ephesians 4:13.
6. Romans 8:18.
7. Henry Vaughan: *The World.*
8. John Bunyan: *The Pilgrim's Progress*, chapter 1.
9. Psalm 90.

Select Bibliography

Athanasius: *Select Works and Letters, Nicene and Post-Nicene Fathers*, Second Series, vol. IV. A Select Library of Nicene and Post-Nicene Fathers, 1886ff.

Augustine: *De Civitate Dei, Nicene and Post-Nicene Fathers*, First Series, vol. II. A Select Library of Nicene and Post-Nicene Fathers, 1886ff.

Barth, Karl: *Church Dogmatics*, I:1,2; II:1,2; III:1,2,3,4,; IV:1,2,3, T. and T. Clark, 1956–1975. *Commentary on the Epistle to the Romans*, Oxford University Press, 1977.

Basil: *Nine Homilies of the Hexaemeron, Nicene and Post-Nicene Fathers*, Second Series, vol. VIII. A Select Library of Nicene and Post-Nicene Fathers, 1886ff.

Boulad, Henri, S. J.: *All is Grace: God and the Mystery of Time*, SCM Press, 1991.

Coveney, Peter, and **Highfield, Roger**: *The Arrow of Time*, Flamingo, 1991.

Dunne, J. W: *An Experiment with Time*, Faber and Faber, 1939.

Ellul, Jacques: *What I believe*, Eerdmans and Marshall, Morgan and Scott, 1989.
Gregory of Nyssa: *Select Works and Letters, Nicene and Post-Nicene Fathers*, Second Series, vol. V. A Select Library of the Nicene and Post-Nicene Fathers (1886ff).

Grosseteste, Robert: *De Cessatione Legalium; De Luce; Hexaemeron*, text by Dales and Gieben, Oxford University Press for the British Academy, 1982.

Hawking, Stephen: *A Brief History of Time*, Bantam Press, 1991.

Irenaeus: *Against Heresies, Ante-Nicene Fathers*, The Edinburgh Edition of the Ante-Nicene Fathers, 1867ff. *Demonstration of the Apostolic Preaching*, Translated by Armitage Robinson, SCM Press.

Kierkegaard, Soren: *Christian Discourses*, trans. W. Lowrie, Oxford University Press, 1961.

McEvoy, J: *The Philosophy of Robert Grosseteste*, Clarendon Press, 1986.

Sorabji, R: *Matter, Space and Motion: Theories in Antiquity and Their Sequel*, Duckworth, 1988.

Southern, R: *Robert Grosseteste, The Growth of an English Mind in Medieval Europe*, Clarendon Press, 1988.

Torrance, T. F: *Christian Theology and Scientific Culture: The Ground and Grammar of Theology*, Christian Journals Limited, Belfast, 1980; *Theology in Reconciliation*, Geoffrey Chapman, 1975; *Theology in Reconstruction*, SCM Press, 1965; *God and rationality*, Oxford University Press, 1971; *Space, Time and Incarnation*, Oxford University Press, 1969; *Space, Time and Resurrection*, The Handsel Press, 1976; *Theological Science*, Oxford University Press, 1978; *Transformation and Convergence in the Frame of Knowledge*, Christian Journals Limited, Belfast, 1984; *Divine and Contingent Order*, Oxford University Press, 1981; *The Trinitarian Faith*, T. & T. Clark, 1981.

Index

of Subjects and Names